About the Author

Rod Nichols started his professional marketing career in 1977 with IBM as an intern. After completing his undergraduate degree in business, he launched into a career with Motorola. In 1983 he left Motorola to start a corporate training and consulting company. During that time Rod formed one of the first monthly networking breakfasts, conducted over 100 seminars, and promoted top speakers such as Denis Waitley and Tom Hopkins.

Rod was introduced to network marketing in 1979 and fell in love with the industry. He has worked with a number of companies and distributor groups as a distributor, consultant, trainer, and author. As a distributor Rod has built several large networks, resulting in full-time income for he and his family. He has trained thousands of network marketers both in person and through his written materials. His recently published recruiting booklet, *Would You Like to Dig in My Goldmine?*, has helped hundreds of network marketers recruit without fear of rejection. Rod also publishes a monthly newsletter entitled, *NETWORKER*, that is packed with information for network marketers.

Acknowledgments

This is a book that I have been researching since 1979, when I was first introduced to network marketing. I would like to extend my deepest thanks and appreciation to a number of people who have made special contributions to this project:

Karen, my wife, who through the years has unconditionally loved, supported, inspired, and believed in me.

Jeff, Lisa, Sara, Cassi, and Willie, my kids, who have put up with all my crazy ideas, night meetings, hours on the computer, and our lack of financial security.

My parents, Frank and Sally, who continue to believe in me.

Mark, my brother, who encourages me to write.

Mr. Mason, my creative writing teacher at Thomas Jefferson High School, who told me I could be a great writer some day.

My best friend, Skip, who is always there for me.

Jay Primm, Marc Barrett, Dennis and David Clifton, Mark Yarnell, Richard Kall, Dave and Coni Johnson, Dave Johnson, Jr., Mary Averill and Bud Corkin, Debbie and Jerry Campisi, Robert Allen, Dallin Larsen and all the other top network marketing distributors who have helped enhance my knowledge of this great industry.

Erin Wait and Karen Billipp for the assistance in promoting this book to the publisher and for the countless hours of editing and revising.

Introduction

Network Marketing Defined

What is network marketing? Actually, every person in the United States has been involved in network marketing for many years, they just don't know it. You have probably read a good book, eaten at a great restaurant, or gone to an excellent movie. Did you tell anyone? If you did, then you are a network marketer. The only problem is that you never got paid to help promote that book, restaurant, or movie.

Network marketing is simply the movement of products or services from the manufacturer or producer to the end user via word of mouth marketing. It is conversational marketing. For example, you use products that are typically better than those you can find in a retail store. If you like them and get results, you tell other people. If they also want to use a product, you make arrangements with your company to get it for them. In exchange for making this arrangement, your network marketing company will pay you a commission, usually at least 25%.

Multi-Level Marketing Versus Network Marketing

Many people ask what the difference is between multi-level marketing (MLM) and network marketing. Some people in the marketing industry say they are the same thing, and others say they are different. The table on page xi illustrates this difference.

The key difference is how marketers align themselves with the parent company. In MLM, multiple levels of people buy products from each other and get paid by each other. Amway and Shaklee are good examples of MLM companies. Only distributors who have reached a leadership level are contracted directly with the company to purchase products and receive checks. Everyone below buys from the leader at a slightly higher price, which results in a wholesale profit for the leader. The company pays bonuses to the leader, and the leader redistributes to the distributors below.

Network marketing is different. Everyone who signs up is contracted directly to the company. They all purchase products directly from the company at the same price and receive their bonus checks directly from the company. The arrangement is closer to franchising than MLM. This system eliminates the need for big inventories and sophisticated bookkeeping systems, thus saving the new network marketer both time and money.

Illegal Pyramid Schemes

One of the most common questions you will hear is, "Isn't this one of those pyramid schemes?" When it comes right down to it, all businesses are pyramids. The person at the top of the pyramid makes the most money, and the workers at the bottom do the work and make a little bit of money. Do all the workers have the opportunity to rise to the top? Yes, one at a time. The government is a pyramid. Our school system is a pyramid. There is nothing wrong with a pyramid. It is one of the strongest structures in the world.

What these people are really asking is, "Isn't this an illegal pyramid?" According to Washington state law, a business venture is an illegal pyramid if a person must make an investment to get the right to recruit others into the program, and if a person receives monetary consideration for recruiting people, and if the new recruits must also make an investment and receive monetary consideration for getting people to join. All three of these requirements must be met in order for it to be illegal. A good example of an illegal pyramid is the chain letter where you send $5 to each of the five listed names, move everyone up, put your name in the #5 slot and mail out 1,000 flyers. There is an investment (with nothing of value received in exchange) and

Multi-Level Marketing versus Network Marketing

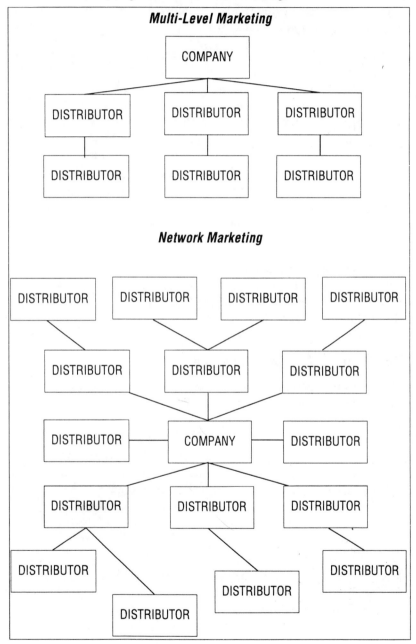

monetary consideration for recruiting. All 50 states have laws and regulations regarding multi-level or network marketing. Check with your State Attorney General's office.

A legal MLM or network marketing company will offer a legitimate product, which can be sold to earn a retail profit. The company will also allow people to recruit or sponsor other people into the program. Marketers receive no compensation until people buy products from the company, whether for their own use or to sell. Typically, people joining an MLM or network marketing company will purchase a starter kit, which contains training materials, brochures, forms, and video and audio tapes. The contents of this kit must be worth at least the cost of the kit and should not contain products. The requirement to purchase a large inventory of products up front is called "front loading" and is considered to be an investment by the State Attorney Council, which may make the company an illegal pyramid.

It is best to look for a company that stresses the distribution of products. This type of company lessens its chances of being investigated, as a possible illegal pyramid, by the State Attorney General or scrutinized by the media.

The Future of Network Marketing

Business analysts such as Robert Allen, author of *Creating Wealth* and Wayne McIlvaine, consultant and former marketing director for McCann Erickson advertising agency, agree that network marketing is the wave of the future. Economist Paul Zane Pilzer, author of *Unlimited Wealth*, expects network marketing sales to double every three to five years. The Direct Selling Association indicates that the direct selling industry accounts for annual sales of 50 billion dollars a year of which network marketing contributes approximately 10 billion dollars. In the May 1990 issue of *Success* magazine, senior editor Richard Poe wrote an article entitled "Network Marketing . . . The Most Powerful Way to Reach Consumers in the 90's." In March 1991, *Success* showcased network marketing in an eight-page article. The publisher of *Success*, Scott DeGarmo, sees network marketing as one of the growing home-based industries and has authorized a monthly column on the subject.

Other business analysts such as Burke Hedges, author of *Who Stole the American Dream*, are comparing the growth patterns of network marketing to those of franchising. Over 30 years ago franchising was a revolutionary new system that people hated. The media called it a scam and rip-off. The papers were filled with stories about people who had lost their life savings in a franchise. Major Fortune 500 companies involved in franchising tried to conceal their identity. Hedges, in his book, indicates that there was even a strong movement by Congress to outlaw franchising. Today franchising contributes over one-third of the Gross National Product.

Why the change? A man named Ray, with a dream. He dreamed about hamburger restaurants with golden arches in every city throughout the U.S. Ray believed in that dream and went on the road to sell it. He sold his initial franchises for $500 to $1,000 each, and many people turned him down saying it was a pyramid scheme. In hindsight, how many of those McDonald's franchises would you have bought?

Business consultants such as Marc Barrett are saying that network marketing is where franchising was about 15 years ago, going into its second stage of growth. During this stage, the network marketing industry will experience popular growth or momentum. During the popular growth stage, an industry becomes so popular that almost everyone is impacted in some way or another. It is during this stage that network marketing, now being called the people's franchise by nearly all involved, will eclipse franchising. It will become the most powerful way to reach consumers in the 90s and beyond.

A Service-Based Economy

One reason for the bright future of network marketing is the U.S. evolution from a production-based to a service-based economy. Network marketing is the growth industry of the future because it best fits this emerging society. More people now work in the white collar segment of the economy than in the blue collar. Economists such as Paul Pilzer say that distribution is the secret to wealth in the future. A service-based economy depends on efficient distribution. Network marketing is the easiest way for average people to get involved in distribution.

Cocooning

Best selling author Faith Popcorn discussed in her book, *The Popcorn Report*, a number of new trends that are changing the face of business. Several of these will contribute to the growth of network marketing. The first is called "cocooning." More and more Americans are seeking the comforts of their home, auto, and office cocoons. The rise in the number of home-based businesses — CNN reported in 1993 that a home-based business is started every 60 seconds in the U.S. — shows how dramatically the cocooning phenomenon is affecting American business. Home delivery, television shopping networks, mail order shopping, and now online computer shopping make it possible for people to accomplish many of their daily chores without leaving their homes. People don't want to fight the traffic or the crowds at the stores. They would prefer to pick up the phone, mail, or fax an order, or touch a few keys on their personal computer to order the things they need and want. The products are delivered safely to their door and generally offer a no question, 100% money back guarantee. This is exactly what network marketing companies offer — a color catalog full of high quality products that can be ordered toll-free on your credit card and will be delivered within a couple of days 100% guaranteed.

Cashing Out

You can find even more evidence that Americans will turn to network marketing as a popular new career choice. Faith Popcorn writes about how the baby boom generation, because of the glut of middle management and corporate downsizing, is cashing out. They are leaving the corporate world by the tens of thousands to start home-based businesses, to experience less work-related stress, and to spend more time with their families. They are seeking time freedom and financial security. Because baby boomers number 76 million in the U.S. and one billion worldwide, a baby boomer flight from the corporate world is a major phenomenon that will last for several decades.

Why Network Marketing?

Why are so many of the boomers choosing network marketing? Consider some of these benefits:

- A home-based business;
- A business with national and international scope;
- A business involved in distribution — one of the most important facets of a service-based economy;
- Minimal start-up costs;
- *Almost* no risk;
- A business you can operate part- or full-time
- A business with no employees and minimal overhead; and
- The possibility of financial security and the time freedom to enjoy life.

What other business offers this list of benefits? Most network marketing companies offer comprehensive training and support, so you don't even need to know how to run a business. Network marketing offers you a way to take control of your financial future. When you work for someone else you get paid what other people think you are worth. You trade your time for other people's money. Unfortunately, you don't have enough time to make enough money to create long-term financial security or any level of time freedom.

A traditional job or business only allows you to earn money based on your efforts, or the efforts of a few closely managed employees — a salary, hourly wage, or profits. Network marketing offers you the ability to leverage your time by finding other people to work with you. If you build a large network, you can earn bonuses based on the efforts of thousands of downline distributors. The best part is that you don't have to invest any more time, this is called "time leverage." Your sponsor, the person who introduced the network marketing opportunity to you, will help you become successful, and you will in turn do the same for the people you sponsor.

Many distributors consider network marketing to be an excellent personal growth experience. As a network marketer, you will learn how to run a successful small business, how to work with all types of people, improve your communication skills, learn to speak in public, establish some successful habits, and have a heck of a lot of fun all the while. Network marketing is challenging, rewarding, difficult, and, at times, frustrating. But you will probably have more fun and meet more great people in network marketing than in all your years in the corporate and traditional business world.

How to Use This Book

Most people purchase a book, read it, and put it up on the book shelf. You will want to use this book differently. It was written as a reference guide for the new and serious network marketer. Read the book completely, making notes regarding areas that would help you build your business. Then keep it handy for regular reference. Here are some ideas for using this book to build a large and prosperous business:

1. Marketing Ideas — there are many great ideas in the book. Pick out two or three that will work for your business and then keep the rest for future use. Network marketing is very much like traditional business in the sense that marketing concepts and techniques don't always produce the same results. When something stops working, refer to this book for new ideas.

2. Training — this is one of the most complete training manuals available, plus it is lower in cost than other training manuals. Use the different sections to develop training programs for your downline. You may even want to include a copy in your new distributor start-up kit. If you are making big bucks and feel generous, give a copy to them. Otherwise, include the cost in their start-up costs.

3. Idea Generator — make sure that everyone in your network (both upline and downline) have copies. That way you can meet or have conference calls to generate new marketing ideas. This book will help you and your network develop productive and profitable new ideas.

4. Motivation — network marketing is a tough industry. You will have to endure a great deal of criticism and rejection. Daily motivation will be critical to your success. This book will help you stay motivated and excited about this industry.

If you are using this book properly, within a few months it should be pretty battered — pages dogeared or paperclipped, Post-it® notes hanging out from important pages, notes and ideas written throughout the book. This is a work book, not a casual reading book. It holds the secrets of success in network marketing. Use it correctly and it can lead you to whatever level of success you seek.

Chapter 1

Choosing the Right Company

How to Recognize the Right Company

If you have already chosen a company, this chapter will help you make certain that you are with the right company. If you haven't chosen a company yet, then this chapter will help you do so.

Thousands of network marketing companies are currently operating, and new ones sprout up every day. Unfortunately, most of them will fail. According to network marketing consultant, Mark Yarnell, "ninety-percent of multi-level marketing companies are bankrupt in the first eighteen months."

Imagine starting your network, recruiting some of your friends and family, and coming to depend on your network marketing income. After about a year, your network really begins to grow, and you enjoy big bonus checks. Then one month your check is late. Rumors start to fly that the company is in trouble. The next month, you don't receive a check. Then you get a notice of bankruptcy from the company. You now have nothing to show for your time but a bunch of mad friends and family members.

Don't jump into the first network marketing company that comes along. It is important that you do your homework. Pretend you are planning to invest a million dollars in this company. Would you do it blindly? Of course you wouldn't. You would spend time investigating the company. You need to do the same with network marketing companies. Check their Dun & Bradstreet rating. Talk with people who have been with the company for a while. At minimum, you want a company that displays the following ten characteristics:

- Has been in network marketing for at least two years, preferably five years;
- Has a management team that has experience in network marketing, is aggressive, and yet fiscally conservative;
- Sells products that are consumable and of higher value than those currently available in retail stores or through mail order;
- Is debt free;
- Makes less than $50 million in annual wholesale revenues;
- Provides excellent training and marketing materials;
- Supplies network communication systems, such as voice mail or satellite hookups for viewing meetings and conferences;
- Arranges for all distributors to buy directly from the company;
- Pays bonus checks directly from the company to all distributors; and
- Has planned for international growth.

If your company or the company you are considering has all of these characteristics, you have probably joined a reputable organization that will contribute to your success as a network marketer. The remainder of this chapter discusses company and network organization in more detail, highlighting why these ten characteristics are so important.

Organization and Compensation Plans

As a network marketing distributor, you want to be directly aligned with your company. In other words, even though you have a sponsor, your agreement should be with the company. This arrangement is very similar to franchising. You sign an agreement that authorizes you to purchase products directly from the company, at a wholesale price, and then sell them for a profit. You can use the company name and logo. You get bulk purchase discounts on marketing and training materials. Most companies provide professional-looking color marketing materials for a small fraction of what you would pay in the open market.

You purchase products directly from the company, rather than from your sponsor or upline leader. This direct purchasing reduces the need for you to build up large inventories. Many network marketing companies offer an even better arrangement. Your customers order products out of a catalog, directly from the company, who in turn ships them directly to your customer. You get credit for the order and receive a commission check for the difference between the retail and wholesale prices.

The company should issue bonus checks directly to all distributors. That eliminates much of the bookkeeping you might otherwise have to deal with. Bookkeeping is generally very minimal in network marketing.

A successful company will have a compensation or marketing plan that rewards people for the movement of products. As was discussed earlier, if it pays you to recruit, then you are in an illegal pyramid. Bonuses should always be based on distribution volume. Also beware of companies whose compensation plans encourage people to invest a large amount of money up front.

An effective compensation plan will reward hard work. The more you sell and recruit, the more you get paid. However, it should also have small rewards for the average, part-time networker. Your new recruits should be able to make money in their first couple of months or they will lose interest. On the other hand, if you are willing to work very hard, be persistent and build a large network, you may someday earn as much as $100,000 per month or more. There are even top distributors in some of the older companies such as Amway, Shaklee, and NuSkin that earn over $500,000 a month. However, these are the exception rather than the rule.

Companies offer many different types of compensation plans, and this chapter only reviews four of the most common. No matter what plan your company offers, be sure to weigh its pros and cons carefully to assure that you will benefit the most from it.

In network marketing, you will have a sponsor who recruits you to join their network. You may also have upline leaders, identified by different titles, such as executive, supervisor, or manager. Sponsors and upline leaders are just individual distributors who have worked hard and qualified to be leaders, which entitles them to earn a higher commission on their network's sales. How your network is constructed, how quickly you can become a leader, and the size of the sales commission you earn from your network's sales is called a compensation plan. The following four plans illustrate how a network or compensation plan is constructed more graphically.

A Breakaway Plan

In a breakaway plan, you can sponsor as wide as you want and generally get paid on unlimited levels of distributors. Everyone joins your network at the same level beneath you — you are their sponsor and, if you have met certain qualifications, their upline leader. They must, by reaching certain levels of personal and group sales volume, earn their way to management levels. Once a person becomes a manager, his or her group becomes a breakaway group.

The breakaway system is much like franchising. You are the franchisor, and you go out to sell your dream to others. Those who join your network and go on to become managers are like mini-franchises. Up until that point, you are responsible for training and support of the entire network. Once a new manager breaks away, he or she is responsible for training and support for that new breakaway network. The new manager also receives the management compensation you were receiving. However, you receive a breakaway bonus, or commission, on that group's sales for life. Table 1.1 illustrates how the breakaway plan works.

To help you understand how you earn money in a breakaway plan, imagine that you join XYZ Company that has a traditional stairstep breakaway plan. You enter as a distributor and buy your products directly from the company. When you sell the products, you earn a 50% profit. After you have developed a good base of retail customers — customers you will need to maintain sales volumes later — you begin recruiting some people. For each person you recruit, you earn a 5% commission on their purchases, called a 5% override. In other words, if they purchase $100 from the company, the company pays you a $5 bonus. The person you recruit is earning the same 50% profit on products sold to retail customers, so they are reselling that same $100 worth of product for $150 to their retail customers.

Table 1.1: The Breakaway Plan

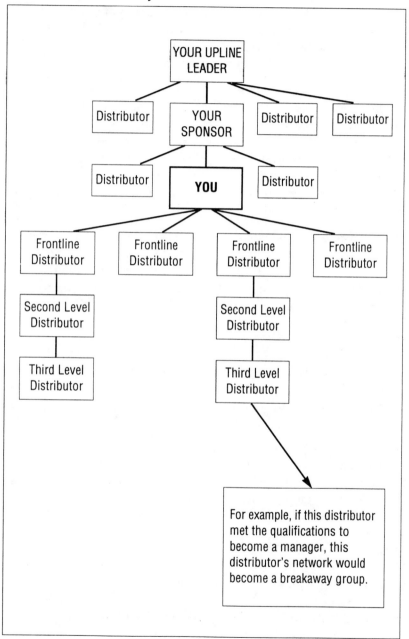

When the people you recruit, called your frontline, are ready to start recruiting people themselves, you do not earn anything from the lower level distributors' sales. These distributors are considered to be on your second level down, and you do not earn bonuses on sales volume beyond your frontline until you become a leader.

To become a leader, you go through a qualification process — you build a larger network, maintain certain personal volumes, and meet group volume goals established by your company. As a leader, you can earn 10% from you first level distributors' purchases, and an additional 15% on your entire group volume. Again, all of these bonuses are paid by the company. When they receive purchase orders from distributors in your network, they record the order and log the bonus due to you in their computer.

Using some of the following conservative estimates, you can roughly calculate the kind of income you, as a part-time network marketer in a breakaway plan, can enjoy. These estimates are based on average sales and recruitment statistics for a leader with one to three years of experience who works part time, 10 to 15 hours per week.

- You become a leader.
- You recruit 30 people on your front line. On average, your frontline purchases a total of $2,000 in product from the company each month. You earn 10% of your frontline's volume, or $200 per month.
- Each of your frontline distributors recruit, on average, two to three people, so that your entire group volume is $4,500. You earn 15% of your group's volume, or $675 per month.
- If you combine your frontline and group volume bonuses, you earn $875 per month in group bonuses alone. If you continue to retail products to your core customers, your annual income could easily be as high as $11,000.

However, as your distributors build their networks, they too will want to qualify to become leaders. When they do, their volume is no longer included in yours, and all management of their network is relinquished to them. Consequently, they receive the leadership bonus of 15% and you receive a breakaway bonus of 5% of their group volume.

At first, this will seem like a cut in pay, which it is. However, over the long run you will build a much larger network and a more secure income when your distributors break away to build their own networks. You can compare the difference to earning 15% of the revenues from one McDonald's restaurant or earning 5% from all the McDonald's in a large city.

One key benefit to a breakaway plan is that everyone in the network is treated equally. Each new distributor has an equal opportunity to achieve. Those who get in early have no more benefit than those who join the company later. Also, most breakaway companies will pay bonuses on three to seven levels of management groups, or mini-franchises. You get paid on many more levels of distributors than in a matrix.

A disadvantage to a breakaway program is that you have to work harder and wait longer to make money. You will not make much money when your network is small. For example, in the beginning, before you become a leader, you only earn the 5% override for distributors you recruit. If you sell $200 in product each month, earning 50% profit, or $100, and you have only five distributors who purchase collectively about $300 in product each month, your monthly income will only be $115. You will have to build a network over a three- to five-year period to tap into the really big income potential.

Also, you will probably have to maintain minimum personal and group volumes to keep your management level. For example, common sales volume minimums are $100 per month for you personally, and $2,000 per month for your group. Many people view minimum sales requirements as a negative because they force the manager to work harder to keep their management status. For the achiever who doesn't mind hard work, minimums are a positive because they stimulate distributors to increase their volumes, which improves overall group volumes.

In a breakaway program, leaders have been known to make $100,000 per month, or more. However, these are people who work at their business full time and have developed very large networks. The average person will earn several hundred to several thousand dollars per month.

If you are an achiever, willing to work hard over the long term to earn the bigger monthly bonuses later, you want to join a company with a breakaway program. All of the top companies, rated by years in business and total annual volume, use breakaway plans — Amway, Shaklee, NuSkin, Herbalife, and Mary Kay. If you want to earn quick money and are willing to take a risk, try a company that operates with a matrix plan.

A Matrix System

If you operate under a matrix marketing plan, you are limited in your frontline recruiting. Companies can construct various types of matrixes, such as a 5 x 5 or 2 x 12. For example, in a 5 x 5 matrix you can only recruit five people on your front line. Anyone else whom you recruit will be placed on your next available level that is not full. You will receive bonuses on five levels of distributors, or on the group volume.

A matrix system is difficult to illustrate, but Table 1.2 can help you understand how a 5 x 5 matrix works. Table 1.2 illustrates the matrix of Brenda' sponsor, Gary. Brenda is on level one of Gary's matrix.

Companies that use a matrix plan may either pay bonuses based on a declining percentage per level or a consistent percentage per level. As an example, if the company represented in Table 1.2 pays on a declining percentage basis, Gary, Brenda's sponsor might earn 10% on all the product Brenda purchases from the company. The distributors that Brenda has recruited are on Gary's second level, so Gary earns only 8% on their volume. However, these distributors, Kristi, John, Jake, Will, and Linda, are all on Brenda's front line. Because they are on Brenda's first level, she earns 10% for all the product they purchase from the company.

Brenda has filled her front line. In a 5 x 5 matrix, Brenda cannot have more than five distributors on her first level. If Brenda recruits an additional person, she will have to place that person on her second level, below either Kristi, John, Jake, Troy, or Linda. Because the company pays declining percentages per level, Brenda will only earn 8% on people in her second level. In fact, Brenda did recruit Bob and

Table 1.2: The Matrix Plan

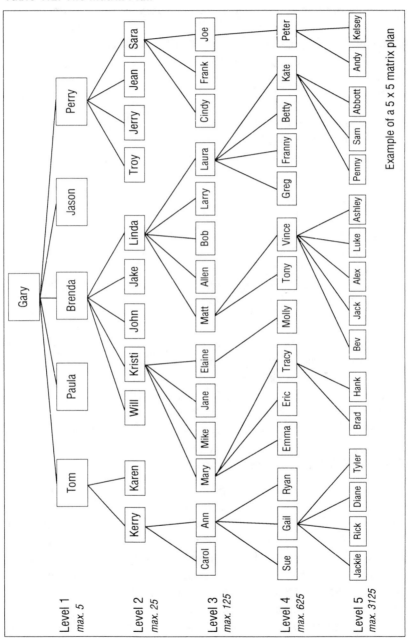

Example of a 5 x 5 matrix plan

decided to place him on her friend Linda's front line because Linda has turned out to be one of her best distributors. Bob is now on Gary's third level, so Gary earns 6% on all product Bob purchases from the company. Brenda earns 8% on product Bob purchases, and Linda earns 10% on product Bob purchases.

Linda has not yet filled her front line. She only has four distributors on her first level, Matt, Allen, Bob, and Laura. If she recruits one more person, she will place that distributor on her first level. If she continues to recruit people, she will have to place them on her second level, below one of her frontline distributors, such as Matt, Allen, Bob, or Laura.

A reminder of one of the most important principles in network marketing — you want your distributors to enjoy some success early on, or they will give up and drop out. If Linda does fill her first level and begins recruiting people for her second level, she may want to pass these new recruits on to Allen or Bob, who are having trouble recruiting. If they acquire a new recruit with their sponsor's help, they may feel motivated to do more recruiting on their own.

However, this strategy can also backfire in a matrix system. Allen or Bob may also realize that they don't have to do any work to acquire distributors on their first level. They may decide not to do any work and let Linda find recruits for them. People like this, who sign up in network marketing but then fail to put any effort into retailing or recruiting, are called "dead wood." These types of people can be particularly dangerous in a matrix system. If Allen or Bob never recruit any distributors, Linda will never fill her second level. Her other frontline distributors may continue to sell and recruit, but Linda will earn a smaller percentage for each level down.

For example, Brenda is experiencing some problems in her frontline. John, Jake, and Will have all become dead wood. They signed up to be a part of Brenda's network, but never recruited anyone and have now also ceased to sell products. Brenda recruited Bob, but she could not place him on her frontline. She had to pass him down to her second level. She will have to wait a year before she can force John, Jake, or Will out of her network and replace them with new recruits who may perform better. In every network, about 20% of distributors turn out to be dead wood. They never sell or recruit. In a breakaway plan, these distributors will not greatly affect a leader's bonuses. In a matrix plan, these people can have a devastating effect.

Very few distributors actually achieve a full matrix. In the process of eliminating the dead wood and moving distributors from lower levels to higher levels, Gary's fifth, sixth, and seventh levels will probably never be filled. In addition, because a matrix system can expand exponentially, if all of Gary's seven levels were filled five across, Gary's fifth level would have 3,125 people, and Gary's entire network would contain nearly 4,000 distributors. Only the top performers will have networks that large.

Nonetheless, a matrix system can produce large incomes quickly. For example, Gary has been building his network for eight months and has recruited 15 people. However, because of recruiting both above and below him, Gary has 55 people in his network on four levels. His monthly bonus is $350. If this had been a breakaway plan, Gary's monthly bonuses would probably be only $45.

One of the key benefits of a matrix system, and one that is promoted quite heavily, is that you don't have to recruit many people. Your upline sponsors will be sponsoring people under you because they can only sponsor five on their frontline. If they can sponsor people below you, they will not earn as much as you will, but they will earn something, so it is to their benefit to help you build your network.

Now, consider the downside of a matrix. Because you are limited on your frontline sponsoring, your successful recruiting will not bring you big bonuses. During the initial excitement, you may sponsor a bunch of people, but after a while you will realize that you are not getting enough benefit, so you will slow down. On the other hand, if a person who is not really ambitious anyway sees an opportunity to have their aggressive sponsor build a network for them, they will quit working. You loose the income potential on that distributor's leg of your matrix.

Matrix organizations usually grow and produce income more quickly than breakaway programs. However, they also crash more quickly. Very few matrix companies have ever survived more than five years, and none, to date, have become billion dollar businesses. One of the most successful matrix companies in 1985 markets nutrition, personal care, and home cleaning products. Your odds of big success with a matrix company are much lower than with a breakaway company.

Two Up or Australian

Another type of compensation plan developed early on in network marketing, in less competitive times, is called the two up plan, or Australian plan because it originated in Australia. The two up plan requires that the first two people you sponsor be passed upline to your sponsor. Every person you recruit from that point goes in your downline, and, of course, their first two recruits will come to you.

A benefit to the two up plan is that your downline, people who are sponsored in your organization after you, will help build your frontline, along with those people you personally sponsor. The problem with this plan is that you may pass your two best people upline, to your sponsor, and then the people you recruit after that don't sponsor anyone. Greed may effect a network as people delay recruiting their best prospects and pass recruits with less potential to their sponsor.

Less than ten companies use this type of plan, and so far no company using the two up plan has become highly successful. This plan will not lead to long-term success. To be successful in a two up plan, you will have to recruit 50 to 100 people.

The Binary or Cellular Plan

The newest type of plan is the binary or cellular plan. This system is a spin-off of the matrix plan, but without the negatives. In this type of plan, you are limited to the number of first level distributors you can sponsor, but you are paid on group volume with no level limitation. Since the average distributor in network marketing will only recruit 2.3 people, this type of program makes good sense for people who have never been successful or have had limited success in recruiting.

Each program is a little different, but the basis of a binary or cellular program is each distributor recruits only two distributors for their frontline. Any others that you recruit are either placed automatically in your downline, or you may place them yourself at any level you wish. An example of a binary plan is shown in Table 1.3.

Table 1.3: The Binary or Cellular Plan

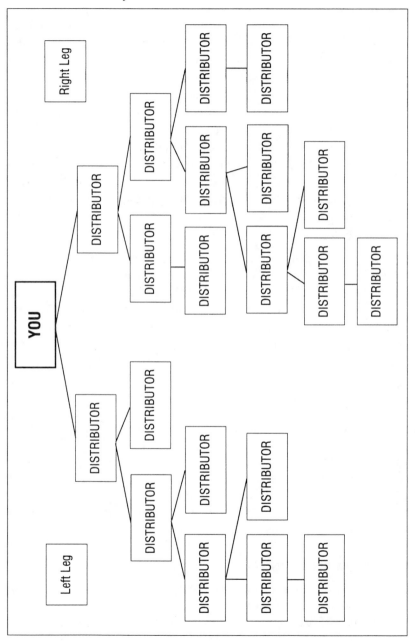

This system creates true networking. Your average distributors have a better chance of making money than in either the breakaway or matrix plans. If you fill your first two positions, you then work closely with those two distributors to help them recruit and sell products. As they recruit, your network grows. You earn bonuses based on group volume, not on levels, so your bonuses are not effected by what level you recruit on. If you want to reward a distributor beneath you, in your downline, you might personally place one of your new recruits in that distributor's network. This kind of reward creates more volume in your network. More importantly, it creates volume for your distributors, which may result in an increase in their sales and recruiting activity. Because you do not face group volume requirements or breakaways in a binary plan, you do not have to worry about missing bonuses or losing your position due to low group volume.

USANA, a company that markets high-end nutritional and skin care products, uses a very effective version of this program. Distributors who have had a difficult time maintaining group volumes in breakaway plans, or have lost good distributors who broke away, have been very successful in the binary or cellular programs. Many of the newer network marketing companies are adopting the binary or cellular plan. This plan will probably be the most popular in the 1990s.

Choosing Your Product

Now that you understand some of the various compensation plans network marketing companies offer, you are ready to focus on some more specific issues involved in choosing the right company. In particular, you need to give some serious thought to the type of product you will sell. Some products sell better via network marketing than others. Specifically, you need to decide between selling products or services, and consumables or nonconsumables.

Product Versus Service

Although many network marketing companies have offered a single service, such as travel, insurance or legal services, only one company has been successful, A.L. Williams, now owned by Primerica, which sells term insurance products. Why? First, not as many services can be marketed effectively through network marketing as can products. Secondly, selling services tends to require people who have specialized sales skills.

Other than A.L. Williams, all of the other top multi-level and network marketing companies offer products. Unless you are a professional salesperson or aspire to be one, you will probably want to go with a company that sells products.

Products are much more viable for network marketing. Remember that network marketing is just conversational marketing. You use a great product, see some personal results, and tell other people. Because you do not have to have any special sales skills, you have much greater growth potential within your network.

Consumable Versus Nonconsumable Products

If you decide to go with a company that offers products, you need to decide if those products should be consumable, such as cleaners, skin care products, or vitamins, or nonconsumable, such as water and air filters, alarm systems, or vacuum cleaners.

High quality, consumable products produce repeat business. If you market a quality consumable product, people will use it up and purchase more. You will have repeat sales every month, so once you have a good group of customers, you will have more time for recruiting. On the other hand, if the product is no better than those on the market, or too much more expensive, people will only buy once and you will have to get new customers every month. The keys to success distributing consumable products are quality and price.

Nonconsumable products are usually more expensive than consumable products, allowing you to make more money on each sale. Most nonconsumables are sold on a trial basis, so you may need to have inventory. Also, nonconsumables typically have a longer life — how often will a person buy a water filter or an alarm system? — so you will need to spend time every month making new sales. Your downline distributors will need to do the same. To succeed with nonconsumable products, you and your network will need to have sales skills and stay motivated to sell every month. Most people do not have sales skills, nor do they want to be a salesperson, so this limits their network size. Again, unless you are a professional salesperson or aspire to be one, stick with a company that has high quality consumable products offered at a good price.

The biggest segment of the U.S. consumer market is the baby boomer segment, consumers between ages 30 and 50 — 76 million consumers in the U.S. alone. Choose a company that is marketing products the baby boomers want and you will increase your odds of success. What do the baby boomers want? — skin care, weight management, hair restoratives, health enhancement, and products that are friendly to the environment. The boomers are environmentally conscious, so they are also interested in water and air purification, and they are conscious of the violent world we live in, so they want security products. Many of these types of products are consumables, and since boomers are buyers of habit, a good consumable product will give you a core group of customers that do their repeat buying with you.

As you begin your research, you will find that nearly all network marketing companies distribute consumable products. Now your task is to find the company that markets products you really like and benefit from. If you see enough value in the products that you would continue purchasing them retail and get excited by the results, then you have found the right products for you.

The Company's Age and Growth Potential

Another issue to consider as you research various network marketing companies is their past experience in network marketing, their current financial status, and their future growth potential.

The Ground Floor Myth

Many people argue that the best situation in network marketing is to find a ground floor opportunity. Everyone wants to get in on the ground floor. If you are smart, you will never get in on the ground floor, unless the new company is backed by an established network marketing company.

If you analyze the ground floor opportunity, you will see how dangerous network marketing can be for a startup company. First, the company is less than two years old, which means statistics show it has a 90% chance of failure. Secondly, it probably does not have many products, quality literature, or marketing materials. Getting in on the ground floor is like being a pioneer. The pioneers came West and took all the Indian arrows, then the settlers came in years later and got the land. Of course a few of the pioneers made it and did well — very few!

You are better off to be a settler and go with a relatively new company — between two and five years old — that is just getting ready to grow. It will have established products and good marketing materials. If you are lucky, it may already have experienced and survived the wrath of legal and media scrutiny.

Old, Established Company Versus Newer, Growth Company

Choosing between an established company and a newer, growing company is difficult. The old, established company offers stability, an excellent product line, outstanding distributor services, and quality marketing materials. However, you have also missed their major growth phase, which means that you may be dealing with some level of saturation — too many people have already been approached and don't want to hear any more about this company or its products. You will need to invest more time to build your business.

The newer, growth company carries more risk because it has a much higher chance of going out of business. It will not offer you the same large selection of products, outstanding distributor services, or quality marketing materials. What it does offer you is a company most people have not heard of and the opportunity to capitalize on their major growth phase. This phase is referred to as the momentum phase. Most companies reach their momentum phase when they enjoy $40 to $50 million in revenues annually. The top companies go from that $40 to $50 million to over $500 million in less than five years. If you can join a company that is about to hit its momentum phase, you can ride this wave of growth.

If you are security minded, stick with the older, established company. If you are ready to take a risk, go with the newer, growth company, but one that meets all the standards established in this chapter.

Management

The management team for a network marketing company can make or break the business. Its members should be young, creative, and aggressive. If they have a great vision for what their company will do for the distributors and the world, they fit the mold.

The company's managers should have experience in network marketing. Typically, managers who have worked successfully in corporate America for years do not make good network marketing founders or managers. Look for a management team that is fiscally conservative. If the company is debt free and has used strictly cash to build their infrastructure, then you have the right type of managers. Also, if the founders are still successfully managing the company, this is a very good sign. Finally, they should be people you feel you can trust and who have the distributor's best interest in mind at all times.

Training and Support

One of the real keys to success in network marketing is proper training and support. Unless you have been successful in network marketing before, don't go into a new venture with preconceived ideas of how you will build your business. Don't reinvent the wheel. Every established company has successful people who will show you tried and true techniques for selling products and building your network.

What may be the most critical factor in your success or failure in network marketing is your sponsor and upline leaders. You need to be sponsored by someone you respect and who is going to work with you to help you build a business. Check out the local support network before you make a commitment. Attend some meetings and trainings to see what level of enthusiasm is generated and to get a feel for the personalities.

Talk with your potential upline people and find out what they are going to do to help you build a business. Will they make three-way calls with you? Will they conduct meetings for you until you are ready to do them yourself? Will they meet one-on-one with your prospects if you are working another job? Will they call prospects for you, participate with you in a cooperative advertising program, or talk with you daily for support and motivation? Your upline and their level of support can make a big difference in your ultimate success as a network marketer.

As you review different companies, check out the distributor kit and training materials. Talk with your potential sponsor about initial and on-going training. Find out what marketing materials are available from the company and other successful distributors. Does the company offer a 24-hour information line, fax-on-demand, weekly tele-conferences, satellite broadcasts, 800 voice mail, video and audio recruiting tapes, or prospecting mailers and packages, including product samples and literature? The more of these materials and services the company or your upline provides, the less time and money you will have to spend to create them.

Financial Status

Most network marketing companies generate phenomenal revenues very quickly. It is for this reason that the financial status of the company is important. If a new company is unprepared for the growth, it will drive them out of business. Many a network marketing company with wonderful products and outstanding, color brochures have gone bankrupt. Check network marketing companies out carefully.

If the company is publicly traded, ask for an annual report. If it is a private company, run a Dun & Bradstreet check on it. Many office warehouse stores, such as Office Max or Office Depot, can run a Dun & Bradstreet report for a minimal fee. You want the company to have the highest D&B rating, which indicates that it has little or no working debt and substantial cash reserves.

If you have trouble getting financial information, call your local Better Business Bureau and your local attorney general to check on the company. If you want to take your research a step further, call the Better Business Bureau and the attorney general in the state where the company is located. They will tell you whether any complaints have been filed against them. Also, you can research the company through the periodical index at the library.

Contact the company and ask for the previous year's annual report or financials. You are looking for indebtedness or signs that the company is slow to pay its vendors or distributors. Check with distributors who have been with the company for a while and ask if their checks arrive on time each month. If you have an opportunity to talk with any of the management team, ask about expansion plans and how new facilities will be financed. If they are not planning to use cash for expansion, chances are good that they will get too far extended if they enter momentum growth.

Next, find out if the company does its own manufacturing or if it pays someone else to perform that function. If the latter, talk with the company and older distributors about the security of the relationship between the company and the facility that does its manufacturing. If the company does its own manufacturing, find out if they own the facilities. Ask how much inventory they keep in stock and how often they experience shipping delays. Determine if they have expansion capabilities so that if the network suddenly doubles they can produce and distribute enough product on time.

Check on the company's other facilities, such as its office, distribution, and research and development. The company's computer system is critical to its long-term success. The computer should be able to track the volume of every distributor and generate a report to an individual distributor that shows the entire downline and their volumes. It should calculate bonuses and issue checks. If the company plans international growth — and it should — the computer should be able to convert currency. The computer should also provide internal and external voice mail and e-mail services to the distributors.

The best situation is to find a company that is debt free, owns its facilities, has pre-paid a great deal of inventory that is sitting in the warehouse, is rated very high by Dun & Bradstreet, and has a fiscally sound plan for expansion.

Hype Versus Genuine Quality

Many companies in this industry rely on hype to move their products. This type of company usually has average products and a poor compensation plan. The founders of these hype companies are just interested in making a bunch of money quickly. They are not interested in the long-term picture or how their plan will affect the distributors.

Beware of the company that hides behind smoke and mirrors. Too much hype indicates that the company is afraid people will see through its scam. It is easy to get sucked into the hype of what appears to be a high growth, ground floor opportunity of tremendous magnitude. All you will really get is a little bit of money and a whole bunch of heartache.

Look instead for a company that uses sound business practices. Their opportunity or business preview meetings will seem no different than a corporate sales meeting. The managers will dress professionally, and quality people will give an exciting, fact-filled presentation, without fanfare or pressure. Then they will allow you to make your own decision based on the information you received.

Growth

Almost all network companies grow. Some grow more quickly than others. Some handle the growth well and others don't. You want to work with a company that has experienced some national growth and is planning or has just started international growth. Make sure your company will allow you to immediately participate in the international growth. Some companies won't let distributors recruit internationally until they have reached a certain level in the company. This may inhibit your growth and cost you thousands of dollars.

Find out how the company plans to expand its product line. A network marketing company has basically two ways for product expansion. First, the company can add new products to the current line, which tends to dilute the line. Second, the company can break into divisions or start new divisions. NuSkin International was the first network marketing company to use this method, to divisionalize. The company started a whole new division to handle a new product line. Divisional diversification offers the financial potential of a ground floor opportunity, but without the risk.

A company will progress through four phases of growth if it is to get very big:

- Formulation
- Concentration

- Momentum
- Stability

During the formulation stage, the company is still in its infancy. It is dealing with product formulation changes and problems. During the concentration stage the company begins to grow rapidly. If it reaches $50 million in annual revenues, then momentum will kick in.

You want to get in at the momentum stage. If you recruit quickly on your frontline and help those you recruit build their frontline for just a few months and capture momentum growth, you can make a fortune.

The stability stage is marked by a large distributor base, annual revenues in excess of one billion dollars, and international growth. Companies in the stability stage have very little growth in the United States because the company is so well known. While you still can make a good deal with a stable company, you will not experience the kind of phenomenal growth you might with a company in the momentum stage.

International Growth

International growth is critical for a company when it moves from the momentum stage to the stability stage. When the U.S. market is saturated by a stable, successful network marketing company, you will have a harder time finding new customers or recruits. However, you can still grow your network by prospecting overseas. Chapter 5 discusses some methods for successful international prospecting and sponsoring.

Beware of companies that are planning very rapid international growth. To properly enter a foreign market takes planning, negotiations, and financial strength. One very large network marketing company recently invested two years of time and over $20 million to enter the Japanese market. However, by properly handling all of the details up front, they were able to open on schedule and do over one million dollars in wholesale revenues in the first week.

If a company is projecting more than one or two new international markets per year, they will likely either experience major disappointment or, at the very least, some serious startup struggles in the new country. In either case, individual distributors suffer when the company receives negative media coverage. Look for a company that is conservative in its international growth projections.

Choosing the right company is very important to your long-term success in network marketing. Take your time and do your research. Don't allow yourself to get pressured or hyped. Look at a number of companies and then make a good, educated decision.

Chapter 2

Success Principles

Traditional Business Versus Network Marketing

Success in network marketing is simple, though not easy, which is why there aren't more successful network marketers. Of course, it all depends on your definition of success. Network marketing success to some is making a few hundred extra dollars each month. To others it is replacing their full-time income. Many people look to financial independence as their sign of success.

In many ways, network marketing is just like any other business. Certain things must be done well, and you need to stick with the business long enough to succeed. However, for the most part, network marketing is the exact opposite of traditional business.

Traditional businesses generally employ a few people to do a lot of work and produce large revenues. In network marketing, you want to build big — recruit many people to work part-time and sell a small amount of volume each, which results in a huge volume for the entire organization. Traditional marketing channels include several layers of middlepeople, each taking a percentage markup. Network marketing eliminates these middlepeople and the costs. See Table 2.1 on page 26 for a comparison of traditional and network marketing distribution.

In traditional sales, you have to learn certain sales techniques and be good at closing sales. Once a prospect says no, your job is to convince them that they really want to say yes. In network marketing, you find products that you love and share the results, or possibly samples, with

Table 2.1: Traditional Business Versus Network Marketing

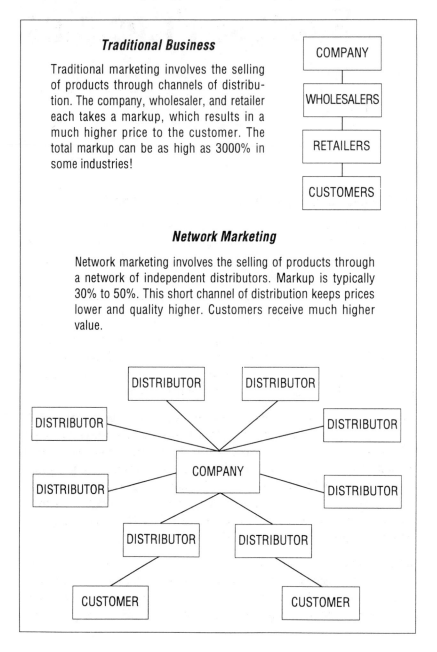

Traditional Business

Traditional marketing involves the selling of products through channels of distribution. The company, wholesaler, and retailer each takes a markup, which results in a much higher price to the customer. The total markup can be as high as 3000% in some industries!

COMPANY

WHOLESALERS

RETAILERS

CUSTOMERS

Network Marketing

Network marketing involves the selling of products through a network of independent distributors. Markup is typically 30% to 50%. This short channel of distribution keeps prices lower and quality higher. Customers receive much higher value.

DISTRIBUTOR DISTRIBUTOR

DISTRIBUTOR DISTRIBUTOR

COMPANY

DISTRIBUTOR DISTRIBUTOR

DISTRIBUTOR DISTRIBUTOR

CUSTOMER CUSTOMER

people you know. They are either interested or not. Either way is okay. You do not need to force a close to the sale or convince your friends or other potential customers to buy.

In traditional business you claw your way up the ladder, keeping all your creative ideas to yourself for fear that someone else will beat you to the top of the corporate pyramid. In network marketing you encourage people to become better than you. You give them all your creative ideas and hope they beat you to the top position in your company, because you earn a percentage of their volume.

Characteristics of the Top Achievers

What does it take to be successful in network marketing? Many people say persistence is the key to success. Others argue that network marketing is a numbers game — if you recruit enough people you will reap big rewards. Others say the key to network marketing is luck — if you recruit a couple of people who turn out to be excellent sellers and recruiters, your bonuses will be big.

All of those are important in different ways. Persistence is particularly important; however, persistence alone is not enough. If you never talk with anyone about your product or opportunity, all the persistence in the world will not make you successful.

When you begin your network marketing career, you want to cultivate certain characteristics in yourself that can contribute to your success. Every career demands certain personality traits. Writers need to be focused and disciplined. Nurses and doctors don't just have to be very well educated in medicine; they need to have good bedside manners as well. Network marketers need to have certain personality traits and human relations skill to excel in their field. The following pages discuss nine characteristics that can help you succeed in network marketing.

Be Courageous

A network marketer must be courageous. From the beginning, you will have difficulty getting support and encouragement in your new venture; you have two strikes against you — you are an entrepreneur, and you have chosen "one of those pyramid schemes." Unfortunately, most people still view network marketing in this way. You must have the courage to weather the storm of this criticism.

Many a network marketer has failed because he or she lacked courage. Be proud of this industry. It is the epitome of the free enterprise system, upon which our great country is built. It is the only true wealth-building system left for the average person. For many people, it is the only way they could ever achieve the American dream.

Be Receptive

Network marketing is a business of duplication. The leaders in your company have already forged the trail, and all you have to do is follow their lead. In order to follow the path, you must be able to take advice and learn methods that work — you must be receptive.

Be Honest

One of the primary reasons that network marketing has such a bad image and reputation is the lack of honesty by a small number of distributors. Be honest with people. Don't show them an upline check for $50,000 and tell them they could be earning that within a few months. First, that is considered to be an inducement and is illegal. Second, it isn't honest and sets them up for failure. Your new distributor will have his or her unrealistic expectations quickly dashed and leave with a bad impression of you, your company, and the whole network marketing industry.

When you are selling products and recruiting people, tell them the truth about the business. Don't exaggerate the facts. Let them know that this is a tough business. They will have to talk with many people to build a network that produces financial freedom. They will experience a great deal of rejection. Products don't sell themselves; people sell products through enthusiasm and excitement.

Most people who look at network marketing aren't going to be interested, and most people who join your network are going to quit — these are realities of this industry. You need to find ways to tell potential distributors and customers about these negatives, while offsetting them with the tremendous benefits of new friends, personal growth, travel, additional income, excellent products to use, time freedom, and financial independence. Chapter 5 discusses many techniques for successful prospecting. The most important one, however, is honesty.

Be a Leader

The world has very few natural leaders, so don't worry if you are not one of them. Many of the top achievers in this industry weren't leaders when they started. They developed their leadership skills while building their business. You learn to be a leader by duplicating what your upline leaders have done to get where they are.

People are attracted to successful people. Become successful in your company and people will follow by duplicating your example. Get excited about your business, even if you don't know much about it yet. Go out and talk with people. Let them see your excitement for the products and business. Working with people and promoting your products will help you learn and build on leadership skills.

Love to Help People

Network marketing requires you to contribute to the success of other people in order to experience success yourself. The more people you help, the more successful your business will be. What is your focus? Is it the money? Stop trying to make money and start making friends. Two very successful network marketers once said that their goal, when they started into network marketing, wasn't to make a million dollars, but rather to make a million friends. In the process they made the million dollars and a whole bunch of friends. Change your focus from surviving to contributing, and you will be amazed at the results.

Be Passionate

The achievers in any industry have a passion for what they do. Their job doesn't feel like work to them. In fact, most of them have a hard time believing they get paid to do what they do. Every network marketing company is filled with people like that. They just love changing peoples lives. Network marketing helps people become more goal-oriented, disciplined, and persistent. Plus, network marketing can dramatically improve your financial position.

If you are not absolutely passionate about your business, products, and company, then you better examine your situation. If you are new with the company, you haven't had enough time to develop passion, so give it time. If you've been with your present company for more than a year and you still have no passion for the product or company, you need to move on. Passion will help you market products and recruit new distributors into your network.

Be Persistent

Any business takes time to build. Unfortunately, most people come into network marketing with a get-rich-quick mentality. They are quickly disappointed when they find that they have to work, and most will drop out.

Building a network that will produce financial independence will take time and hard work. If you are working at your network marketing business full-time and are aggressive, you could conceivably build that network in a year. If you are a part-time distributor putting in 10 to 15 hours per week, you should plan to invest three to seven years to build your network.

You have to understand that you are just a contractor building a very large building, one brick at a time. Each time you talk with someone about your products or the opportunity, you put in a brick. At first, it just looks like a bunch of bricks, but after a while it starts to look like a building. Do the things you need to do, every day. Stick with it long enough and you are bound to succeed.

Have Unshakable Faith

The achievers in this industry have unshakable faith in their company, product, and themselves. No matter what happens — media scrutiny, bad comments from friends and family, or rejection — they continue to have faith in their opportunity to build financial independence and the accompanying time freedom.

It is important for you to work with a company and products in which you can build that level of faith. Your unshakable faith will sell the business opportunity and products more often than any other factor. If your prospects can feel your faith, they are more likely to try your products or participate as a new distributor.

Be Self-Disciplined

One of the biggest reasons for failure in any business is lack of discipline. As an entrepreneur, you won't have a boss telling you what to do. Although your sponsor is there to help, his or her responsibility is not to get you going every day. You will need to set up a daily routine for doing business. If you are working at your business part-time, then scheduling your time is extremely important. As you schedule your week, plan time slots for your networking activities. As a full-time network marketer, your task is to have the discipline to work your business every day as if it were a job. Many people start enjoying the time freedom before their income is stable, and they soon find that they don't have a business.

The remainder of this chapter discusses time planning and goal setting, two important skills for establishing and building your business. You will also find some helpful hints in Chapter 3, Getting Started.

Time Planning

"I never have enough time. There just aren't enough hours in the day." Does this type of complaint sound familiar? Because network marketing is a career that allows you to work independently and without supervision, your success depends on your ability to be your own boss. You need to effectively plan your time for advertising your product, contacting prospects, and building your network. The first step to successful work independence is to build a time planning model.

Develop a Time Planning Model

Technology and changing work methods have forced people to change the way they handle time. People used to focus on getting the most done in a particular moment. Today, people emphasize the need to plan for future goals. So much information enters your life every day that you need to plan for how you will process it in a fixed 24-hour day, or 8-hour work day.

The secret to effective time planning is to have a system. One very effective time planning model is the five-part system outlined below:

- Practice good self-management;
- Have a purpose;
- Set and achieve worthwhile goals;
- Conduct strategic planning; and
- Schedule effectively.

This step-by-step time planning system can help you achieve the self-discipline and leadership skills you need to build your network marketing business.

Time Wasters

Time wasters can destroy your productivity. The only truly productive activity in network marketing is to give a presentation to a qualified prospective distributor or retail buyer. You need to perform many other activities to reach the actual presentation step, but many network marketers spend too much time doing the intermediate steps rather than moving forward to the most important activity, the presentation. Some of the most common time wasters include:

- Daily organizing — As you get more involved in selling and recruiting, you may find it easier and more comfortable to organize your desk and files than to call and prospect people. Unfortunately, people will not call you and say, "I hear you're in network marketing, tell me about it." Every top leader will tell you that to be successful in network marketing, you have to prospect people every day. You need to keep your office organized and files up to date, but make sure you do not spend more than half an hour each day doing it. The rest of the time you should spend prospecting.
- Procrastination — In network marketing, everyone tends to put off prospecting for easier activities, such as talking to your upline or downline, getting marketing materials ready, or designing new marketing materials. The key to success is to determine what is going to

help you reach your goals and achieve your dreams. Make a daily list of things you need to do to move you closer to your dreams. Do those things first, and then do the less important activities. That way, if you run out of time, you still have a productive day.

- Safe phone calls — The safe phone call scenario is common in network marketing. You sit down to make your prospecting calls, the receiver feels like it weighs 500 pounds, so you decide to call your upline, sponsor, distributors, Mom, or best friend. You know these people won't reject you; in fact, they will probably stroke your ego. These safe calls make you feel good, but they don't produce results. If you are going to be successful in network marketing, you need to focus your telephone time on prospecting and following up on prospects.

- Interruptions — As a network marketer, you will most likely work out of your home. You will face many different types of interruptions — door-to-door salespeople, kids, pets, and phone solicitors. These interruptions are time wasters. They cut into your retailing and prospecting time, unless you attempt to sell products to or recruit these people. The more successful you are at handling these interruptions, the higher your level of success in business.

The lifeblood of your network marketing business is people, so you will need to have contact with people on a number of different levels, including product demonstrations, prospecting presentations, interaction with other distributors, conversations with company representatives, and training sessions. People-to-people contact is critical, but on a controlled basis. You will need to learn how to control interruptions. Here are some suggestions:

- Let people know right away that you are busy and don't have time to talk;

- Keep a timer by the telephone and let the other person know that you can only talk for three minutes. When the timer alarm goes off, end the conversation.

- Inform employees, distributors, and sponsors that you can only accept calls during designated times each day.

- Let your voice mail or answering machine answer calls, screen them, and then return the calls when it is convenient for you.

- If you are interrupted by a person at your door, do not allow the person to sit. If you stay standing, the interruption will be much shorter. You can even begin to walk them back to the door as you make some concluding comments, such as "It was nice to see you. We will have to schedule a time to get together again soon."

- Keep the conversation focused on business. Do not allow small talk or gossip to creep in, unless you have the time. If you stay focused, so will the other person.

- A quick glance at your watch or the clock will quite often let your visitor know that you are under a time constraint.

In network marketing, time is your most valuable asset. Learn how to control the time wasters, so that they do not steal your opportunity for network marketing success.

Activity: Time Wasters

List the time wasters in your life and rate them in order of priority, high to low. Once you have your list, answer the following questions;

1. Which of your time wasters are created by you?

2. Which of your time wasters are created by other people or events.

3. How can you control or eliminate these time wasters?

Developing Successful Habits

As you enter the field of network marketing, you will arrive with some bad habits — habits you have developed at home, or habits you have learned from your parents, teachers, or peers. You also have certain beliefs that go along with these habits. For instance, you may have been told that you would never be a good salesperson. Now you have that belief deeply ingrained in your subconscious and you act on it any time a situation arises that even resembles sales.

Keep in mind that network marketing is not sales, though it does resemble it. If you are coming in with the habit of avoiding situations that appear to be sales, you will need to change this habit, or you will inevitably fail. The same goes for public speaking, working with people, or running a business — you need to overcome any fears you have of these activities.

Changing a negative habit is somewhat more difficult than creating a new habit because it requires conscious activity. If you try to avoid the bad habit, you will spend time thinking about it, and your mind will confirm the bad belief and habit. Scientific experiments show that the most effective way to change a habit is to replace the memory. To do this, you must replace the negative memory with a clear picture of the desired result. Earl Nightingale, in *The Strangest Secret*, wrote that we become what we think about most. People who achieve greatness see themselves as great already. Those who try and fail already see themselves as failures.

To be successful in network marketing you must know what you want — you must clearly define your purpose, goals, and objectives. You must have a clear picture of the end result — whether you want wealth, a full-time income, good part-time income, or only a few hundred extra dollars each month. Then you must clearly see the steps necessary to create the end result. Focus on these positive thoughts, and the beliefs and habits will slowly change.

You will need to spend three to five weeks to change a bad habit. The sooner you begin, the earlier you will enjoy the results. Here are some guidelines to help you make the transformation.

- Start your new habit forming activities right away. Think of changing your bad habits as reprogramming a computer. If you had a flawed computer program that caused the computer to produce incorrect data, would you put off fixing it until another day? Of course not, so why treat your life any differently? Begin programming that incredible computer in your head with new, positive habit changing information and responses right away.

- Never let an exception occur! It is easy to let your habit forming activity slip just once, but if you are to succeed, you must not allow an exception until the new habit is firmly rooted, at least 21 days. If you allow even one exception, your computer immediately reverts back to the original programming, and you will have to start over from the beginning. It is not worth the pain and frustration, so don't let the exceptions creep in.

- To create a new habit, you will need to change the way you think about yourself., You must see yourself as you would like to be, rather than as you have been.
- Never doubt yourself.

As you prepare to start your network marketing career, think about the types of habits you would like to have, the bad habits you would like to change, and the habits that will contribute to your success as a network marketer. The following activity, Changing Habits, will help you with that process.

Activity: Changing Habits

1. Choose a negative habit that you would like to change, and that would inhibit your growth in network marketing — for example, procrastination, disorganization, fear of public speaking, fear of meeting new people, or fear of calling people on the phone.

2. Write a statement that describes the end result as you would like it to be, such as standing in front of a group of 3,000 people and giving a flawless speech, with the people cheering and applauding.

3. Determine the steps you need to take to reach this end result.

4. Plan to take these steps over the next 21 to 30 days.

Setting Goals

To achieve your goals, you need to have a clear purpose for setting those goals. All of the top network marketers have a well established purpose for why they are involved in network marketing. Some want extra money, others want freedom from the constraints of a job. For most it is to create time and financial freedom. Quite often, underlying the financial goals is a desire to help other people. Network marketing is a people-helping-people business, so this purpose is achieved by building your business ethically and honestly.

Why is purpose so important? If you have ever found yourself questioning your occupation or an activity, then you probably lacked purpose. If you lay in bed in the morning trying to determine why you should get up, then you lack purpose. If you have ever set a goal, worked hard, but didn't reach it and didn't know why, you probably didn't have a clear purpose.

Goals are critical to your success in network marketing. In your new business, you will have two types of goals. The first are called dream goals — a dream home, dream car, condominium in an exotic place, Rolex watch, airplane, or freedom to travel six months each year are a few examples of dream goals. The second type of goals are activity goals, the daily, weekly, monthly, and yearly goals that will eventually allow you to achieve your dream goals. These goals are like stepping stones on a path to success. The key is that you have to get on the right path and now upon which stones to step.

In network marketing, goals are relatively easy to set. Look at the company's compensation plan to see if the company has set goals for you to reach to receive higher monetary benefits. If not, then create your own goals. Analyze the compensation plan. Figure out how much money you want to make and when. Then determine, based on the compensation plan, what you will need to do to make that amount of money by the date you set.

You now have a goal — to earn a certain amount of money by a particular date. Next, break this down into small goals or objectives to make the larger goal more attainable. For example, you might set a goal to make $25,000 per month from your network marketing business within three years. Look at the compensation plan — work with your sponsor or upline leader if you are having trouble understanding the plan — and determine the sales volume you will need to receive a monthly check of at least $25,000. Then figure out how many distributors you will need to generate that volume, for example, 1,000 distributors. Of course, you do not have to recruit all 1,000; most will be the result of exponential growth during the three years.

In this example, you will need to personally recruit 72 distributors during the three years. That translates into 24 per year, or two per month. You can then figure that to recruit two people per month, you will need to give ten business presentations per month, assuming that 20% will say yes. You can determine you will need to have 100 contacts each month to make ten presentations — three contacts per day, working all 30 days in a month. Since a contact can be a friend, family member, business associate, your insurance or real estate agent, dentist, doctor, grocery store checker, bank teller, or anyone else you meet during your busy days, three contacts per day should be fairly easy.

This example illustrates how easily you can break down a big goal, or dream goal, into smaller, more attainable, daily or monthly activity goals. You will also want to set retailing goals for yourself, such as the number of new customers you reach each month, your retail volume, or the number of new products you sell. As you build your network, your goals will expand into management also. Helping your downline distributors become successful will become a big part of your goals.

The sample goal planner on page 43 will help you set goals for your network marketing business. If you don't know the ratios of contacts to actual presentations, or presentations to successful recruits, ask your sponsor, or use the following industry averages:

- 10% of new contacts will be interested; and
- 20% of people who attend a presentation will become customers or distributors.

Write your goals and review them daily. Modify them as necessary. You may want to make copies of the blank goal planner so that you can use it each year as you build your network marketing business.

Strategic Planning

As you develop and grow your new network marketing business, you may begin to get new offers — your name will get on MLM and network marketing mailing lists, and you will receive information on other network marketing opportunities. However, if you have done your research in the beginning, you will know that the company you chose is the best one for you. A key to success in any business, particularly network marketing, is to stay focused.

The best way to stay focused is to establish a set of goals and a strategic plan for achieving those goals. The following four-step process is an excellent strategic planning tool.

Step 1: Turn Your Goals into Projects

To achieve the highest level of productivity each day, you need to evaluate all potential activities and schedule those that will produce the best results. Divide your activities into two lists. The first, activities that take only one step, such as going to the bank or picking up milk at the store, call your "items to do." The second, more complex, multi-step activities, call your projects.

Projects require more than one step, so planning is critical to their successful completion. An item to do requires only one step and can be planned in your head. In this strategic planning system, you focus most of your efforts on projects and the daily activities necessary to complete the project.

Feelings of crisis are caused by misunderstanding your current workload. Most people operate without a clear understanding of their current obligations. People agree to do things without thinking about how or when they will do them.

Turning your goals into projects and then focusing your daily efforts on those projects will give you clarity and help you decide what you can and cannot do. This clarity will give you the power to delegate, eliminate, restructure, and manage your daily activities so that you will accomplish more in less time.

Step 2: Create the Project

As part of this step, write one of your network marketing goals at the top of a piece of paper. Write a statement, using action verbs, to describe the project. For example, if your goal is to attract 20 new retail customers, your statement might be, "In this project, I will use a number of marketing methods to attract 20 new retail customers.

Step 3: Identify the Key Activities

The next step is to identify the key activities for your project. This can be a difficult step if you try to put these activities in order. The human brain doesn't work this way. Your thoughts are very non-linear, so don't try to record them in a linear outline format. Instead, use a technique called mind mapping, a brainstorming process created by Tony Buzan.

Again, if your project is to attract 20 new retail customers, you would first draw a circle labeled 20 customers in the middle of your project page. Then, draw lines off the circle, like spokes on a wagon wheel, labels with activities that will help you achieve the goal of attracting 20 new customers. The sample project planner on page 45 illustrates this mind map.

Your key activities, listed on the spokes of your mind map, may also stimulate sub-activities, activities that lead to or result in the primary activity. For example, if one of your main activities is to do a product demonstration, some of the sub-activities would be to set up a location, invite people to the demonstration, make up handouts, and ask your upline to assist you. As you build your mind map, add activities and sub-activities until you have all your ideas on paper.

Step 4: List Your Key Activities

Using your mind map as a reference, list the key activities necessary to complete your project. Start each activity statement with an action word — list, do, contact, call, write, mail. After you have completed your list of key activities, put a completion date after each one. This will help you with creating a time-line for the project.

Next, look at each activity and estimate the amount of time it will take to complete. Write that amount of time in front of the activity. This will help you plan your time more effectively each day.

Use the blank project planner on page 46 to turn your goals into activities and strategically plan to achieve those goals.

Items to Do

Along with the key activities from your projects, you will also have items or things to do each day, such as pick up the dry cleaning, drop children off or pick them up from their various activities. These are things you must do, but they do not relate directly to your projects. To help prioritize your projects and your other errands, make a separate items-to-do list. On this sheet of paper, list all the extra errands or chores that arise every day and need to be done. Don't start a new one every day, that is too time consuming. Keep the same list and just mark off the ones you have completed. Use this list along with your project lists to schedule each day.

Priority Scheduling

Scheduling is the bridge between strategic planning and actual results. A plan tells you what to do; a schedule tells you when. Effective scheduling brings you freedom. When you know the truth about what you plan to accomplish, you have the freedom to be effective with each activity. In addition, you will be better able to handle interruptions without losing your focus.

The three areas you will use to establish each daily schedule are:

- Established appointments;
- Project lists; and
- Items-to-do list.

To properly schedule your time, you need a few scheduling tools, including an appointment book with daily scheduling pages, an items-to-do list, project key activity lists, and a monthly calendar.

The first step to priority scheduling is to establish a consistent time each day when you will do your scheduling. If you are a morning person, if you have most of your energy or are most creative in the morning, do your scheduling in the morning. On the other hand, if you work better at night, do your scheduling at night.

The second step is to determine how much time you will budget each day for each of your priority activities — career, family, social life, and self. Obviously your days will vary. The key is to have a basic time budget to work from as you schedule so that you do not waste time.

The third step is to begin scheduling. Each day as you begin scheduling, first review your time budget, project activity list, scheduled appointments, and items-to-do list. Evaluate any potential interruptions or crises that may occur that day. Keep in mind that your project activities hold priority over everything else, since they will help you reach your goals. Identify the priority activities for the day by giving them an "A", next highest priority a "B", and lowest priority a "C.". Then label each activity with the amount of time you project each will take.

Now begin blocking time slots. In other words, if one of your priority activities is to follow up on ten leads, and you estimate that you will need an hour for that activity, then block an hour slot during the time of day in which you feel this project item will be best served. Also, block your appointments and make sure to include enough time for travel, if necessary. Nothing is more stressful than scheduling time slots too close together.

If you find you have more activities than time allotted, review all of the activities and adjust the timelines, think of alternative ways to implement them, or delay them to the next day. Do this until your activities and time frames fit into your schedule. This process is often agonizing, but is quite necessary. It is unproductive to live in pretense about what you can and can't get done in a day. By telling yourself the truth about your time commitments, you will reduce your daily stress and accomplish more in a day than you ever have.

As you develop your network marketing business, try to implement the strategic planning and priority scheduling systems described above. Preventing procrastination and achieving your daily, weekly, and monthly goals will assure that you reach your big goals — a successful business, financial and time freedom, and a personal sense of accomplishment and satisfaction.

Sample Goal Planner

Purpose Statement:

My purpose in network marketing is to achieve financial freedom by helping others do the same.

Goal Statement:

My goal is to have an income of at least $30,000 per month by January 1st.

Objectives:

Find 20 retail customers who purchase at least $50 per month.

Recruit 2 new distributors per month.

Make 3 new contacts per day.

Make 2 new presentations per week, or one group presentation with at least 2 prospects.

Make at least 5 three-way calls per week with downline distributors.

Conduct a new distributor training session every other week.

Affirmations:

I have 20 happy retail customers who are buying at least $50 each month.

I am recruiting at least 2 distributors each month.

I find it easy to make 3 new contacts per day.

I enjoy presenting my business opportunity to at least 2 prospects per week.

I make arrangements for at least 5 three-way calls per week with my distributors.

My bi-weekly training sessions are really helping the new distributors.

Visualization Statement:

It is now January 1st, and my $30,000 check has arrived. It is so great that we haven't even had time to spend the one from last month. We did pay cash for the new furniture and take a trip to Hawaii. This month we are donating half of our check to a local homeless shelter for them to buy food and supplies. $5,000 of the money is going into our investment plan. The rest we will use for household expenses and a quick trip to Sun Valley skiing. Next month, we are buying a new car and paying cash. We are also having plans designed for our dream house.

Activity: Goal Planner

Purpose Statement:

_____

_____

Goal Statement – statement of your goal with a time frame

_____

_____

Objectives – break your goal into smaller steps

_____

_____

_____

_____

_____

_____

Affirmations – positive statements, as if your goal has been achieved

_____

_____

_____

_____

_____

_____

Visualization Statement – how life will be when your goal is completed

_____

_____

_____

_____

_____

_____

Sample Project Planner

Goal:

My goal is to have an income of at least $30,000 per month by Jan. 1.

Mind Map: (to determine objectives)

Objectives: (break the goal into smaller steps)

Retailing:

    2 demonstrations per week

    5 one-on-one's per week

    25 catalogs out per week

Recruiting:

    20 new referrals per week

    10 new names from each new distributor

    5 group presentations per week

    10 one-on-one presentations per week

Marketing:

    3 ads placed per week in newspaper

    Online ads placed on America Online and Compuserve

Activity: Project Planner

Goal:

_____

Mind Map: (to determine objectives)

Objectives: (break the goal into smaller steps)

Retailing:

_____
_____
_____

Recruiting:

_____
_____
_____
_____

Marketing:

_____
_____

Chapter 3

Getting Started

Many people who sign up to be network marketers really don't know what they're getting themselves into. They don't realize that this commitment will require them to start a real business. Lack of commitment is one of the main reasons people drop out of network marketing. If you paid a million dollars for the rights to a McDonald's franchise and capitalized $2.5 million more for the building, equipment, and supplies, would you quit in 30 days? Of course not. You have the building, employees, and equipment that proves you have a legitimate business. Network marketers don't have those things to prove they have a real business. All they have is a distributor agreement, a kit, and a few products. They have no store, no office, no warehouse, no employees, no equipment. However, those are the benefits of network marketing. Even though you don't have a huge investment, you still need to treat it like the big business it is.

Part-Time or Full-Time?

The first step is to decide if you are going to run your network marketing business part-time or full-time. Most people start a network marketing business part-time, but more and more people are jumping from working for someone else right into network marketing full-time. If you are sick and tired of your job and have the financial backing to carry you for at least six months, you may want to consider starting full-time. Sit down with your sponsor and analyze the compensation plan to determine what you would need to do to recreate your full-time income. Then decide whether you are willing to do that.

If you do not have the financial cushion, start your network marketing business part-time. It is a great way to learn the business and make some mistakes without increasing your stress level. If your goal is to work your business into full-time, then have your sponsor or upline leader help you with a sequence of goals that will result in a full-time income. Your first goal should be to get some retail customers and recruit your first distributor. Next, set a goal to make enough to pay for the cost of doing business. Then go for $300 to $500 per month in actual income. After that, you can set a goal to replace your current income so you can go full-time. One suggestion, don't quit your day job, or night job, until your network marketing income is greater than your full-time income for at least three months in a row. Many people new to network marketing get themselves into financial trouble by leaving their job before they have enough business income.

If you are considering a full-time network marketing career, you need to know what it will be like. You will work long hours, recruit all day, attend meetings, and do paperwork in the evenings. You will attend or conduct trainings every Saturday. You get to take Sunday off, unless you happen to run into a great prospect. Mark Yarnell, contributing editor for *Success* magazine and successful network marketing distributor, says that if you work full-time, you should be prospecting a minimum of 30 people per day. You will learn many ways to prospect and contact potential distributors in Chapter 5. As a full-time network marketer, you need to treat your work as a big business and set big goals.

Setting Up Your Business

As a network marketer you are an independent contractor. This means that you own your own business, which represents the network marketing company. One of your first decisions will be the legal form of ownership. As a small business owner, you have a choice of four forms of ownership: sole proprietorship, partnership, C corporation, and S corporation. Some other forms do exist, including, in some states, the limited liability company, but these four are the most common.

Sole Proprietorship

As a sole proprietor, you are the sole owner. You make all the decisions, incur all the expenses, and receive all the profit. Legally, your personal and business assets are not distinguished, but rather considered one and the same. You should, however, keep them separate through your bookkeeping. Because assets are not legally separated, your personal assets may be in jeopardy if your business creditors cannot collect from your business funds.

If you need to have total control over the business, then sole proprietorship is the best option. On the other hand, if you like input on decisions and plan to bring on additional owners, you should consider other legal forms.

In a sole proprietorship, the profits from your business are all yours. However, because you do not have any partners or other owners, you will have to depend on your income and personal credit rating to qualify for business financing.

Partnership

Most small business partnerships are called general partnerships. All partners are general partners, and they each have the same rights and liabilities. Profit from the business is usually divided equally among the partners, and each partner is personally responsible for the liabilities of the business.

A partnership has two main advantages. First, more people can help with problem solving and managing the business. A partnership is not as lonely as a sole proprietorship. Second, because more people are involved, the business will likely have a higher credit rating, provided the partners all have good credit.

However, the disadvantages to a partnership are many. Decisions are sometimes difficult because all the partners need to agree. If all the partners have strong personalities, you may have conflicts over leadership roles. A partner may consciously or unconsciously create a liability for your business. Even though you did not have anything to do with the act or decision, you are still personally responsible.

Pick your partners carefully. Do not go into partnership with someone you don't know well. Make sure that all partners have the same goals and that each has knowledge or skills that will contribute to reaching those goals. Work together for a while before starting the business to make sure you have no immediately evident personality conflicts.

Most importantly, write a partnership agreement outlining the goals of the business, each partner's responsibilities, the method and amount of remuneration, and arbitration methods. You also want to include a section or have a separate agreement covering what happens if a partner is disabled, dies, retires, or wants to leave the business, and what happens if you need to add more partners. This kind of agreement is called a buy and sell agreement because it discusses how partners can buy into or sell out of the partnership.

A partnership is like a marriage. In fact, you may spend more of your waking hours with your partners than with your spouse, so it is important that you pick the right people and put everything down in writing. The most successful partnerships are those between people who have known each other for some time, have been active in similar businesses, and have compatible personalities and attitudes.

C Corporation

A C corporation costs more to start than a sole proprietorship or partnership, but it does offer some special advantages. The best advantage is that a C corporation is a legal entity, so your personal assets are protected from creditors. Creating a C corporation is like creating an artificial person who owns and operates your business and is responsible for all the business' assets and liabilities in the eyes of the law, leaving your personal assets protected from any of the corporation's creditors.

Another big advantage to a C corporation is longevity. Because the C corporation is a legal entity, the life of the business does not end with the death of an owner or stockholder. If you set your business up as a C corporation, you will have an easier time getting commercial financing because lenders will feel more secure about the business' ability to pay over the long term.

Incorporating also has some disadvantages. The first is the cost, which can range from a couple of hundred dollars to thousands of dollars depending on the complexity of the company and whether you use an attorney. You also need to consider taxation. In a sole proprietorship or partnership, the business' income is only taxed once. In a C corporation, the business' income is taxed twice, once within the corporation, and again in the form of salary or dividends you enjoy as an employee or stockholder in the corporation.

Corporations are somewhat constraining in that they are subject to considerable amount of regulation compared to the sole proprietorship or partnership. A corporation must have a board of directors that meets annually. You must keep records for each board meeting. A corporation is also required to complete public disclosure reports and file articles of incorporation.

The articles of incorporation will at very least include the name of the corporation, the promoter's name, the address of the corporate office, a description of the purpose for the corporation, the names and addresses of all incorporators and first year directors, classes of stock, and voting rights.

If you are starting a small business and plan to keep it small, you probably do not want to form a C corporation unless you are in a high risk venture and want to protect your personal assets. If you are concerned about protecting your personal assets, an S corporation may be a better alternative.

S Corporation

The name S corporation was derived from the subchapter S of the Internal Revenue Code, which allows a company to maintain the limited liability features of a C corporation, while being taxed like a partnership. Any income you derive from the company will be placed on your IRS form 1040 as personal income.

The S corporation has some limitations. The laws regarding S corporations change quite often, so check with your state licensing department or your state's edition of The Oasis Press' *Starting and Operating a Business* series. Some of the limitations to an S corporation are listed below.

- The business can have no more than 35 stockholders.
- All stockholders must be individuals or qualifying estates and trusts.
- The corporation can have only one class of stock.

- The business must be a domestic operation.
- The business cannot have nonresident stockholders.
- The corporation cannot own more than 79% of stock in another corporation.

If you are forming a small business and would like to raise start-up capital by selling stock to people you know and have your income taxed at the lower personal rates, then a subchapter S is the form of ownership for you. In fact, unless you plan a huge expansion, subchapter S may be the best form of ownership.

For more information on incorporating, consult The Oasis Press' *The Essential Corporation Handbook*, a comprehensive and up-to-date guide to incorporation, including information on limited liability companies, a new form of business ownership approved in 40 states.

Activity: Form of Ownership

Analyze the four forms of ownership and select the one that will work best for your business. If possible, prior to your selection, talk with owners who are using the different forms to get their input.

Company Name

You will represent a network marketing company, but will not be able to use the company name as a part of your company name. Thus you must choose a name for your business. Many people starting businesses do not take enough time to develop a company name. Although people will not do business with you just because of the name, it can help you gain more business.

Here are some quick tips for creating an effective company name. First, the name should describe what you do. For example, Clear Water might inform customers that you sell water filters, Quantum Security might describe the security alarms you sell, or World Health might explain that you sell nutritional products. Your customers should be able to look at your name and have some idea of what you do; otherwise, some customers will pass you by.

Unless you are planning to stay small and local, do not use names that relate to your region, city, county, or state, such as Seattle Security. If Seattle Security decided to operate in Portland, Oregon, the name would be very inappropriate. You also want to anticipate the possibility of international business. The business world is moving closer to a global economy every day. You never know when that big international opportunity might present itself. It would be too bad if that opportunity passed you by because your name sounded like a little, local business.

You probably do not want to use your own name as a part of your company name. In business you never know what is going to happen. Awful things like lawsuits and bankruptcies happen to nice people. You definitely do not want your good name damaged if your business gets into legal or financial trouble.

Two words are overused in naming network marketing businesses — enterprises and associates. Stay away from both. Unfortunately, because of the overuse, many people who don't understand network marketing may judge your company based on the use of enterprise or associates. They tend to identify those two words with illegal pyramid schemes and will logically think your business fits into that category.

If you are having trouble developing a name, you may find some ideas in the Yellow Pages of your phone book. Of course, you cannot copy another business' name, but you can use some of the words or concepts. Look in the section where your business would be listed if you used Yellow Pages advertising and study the names of your competitors. Keep in mind that your white and yellow page listing is alphabetical. If you are planning to advertise in the phone book, you will appear earlier in the listings if your company name begins with a, b, or c. If you plan to get most of your business through direct marketing or referrals, where your company name appears alphabetically really doesn't matter. Check with the company you represent. Some network marketing companies do not allow distributors to advertise in the Yellow Pages until they reach a certain level of leadership.

Once you have some name ideas, check out all of the area phone books to see if another business uses that name. If you set up a corporation, most states will run a name search. If you operate your business as a sole proprietorship or partnership, you may choose to pay your attorney to do a name search.

Most states require you to register your company name so that another company can't use the same name. Call your local licensing agency about the need to register your company name. If you have a very unique name or are planning a large national expansion, you should trademark your company name. Contact the national patent and trademark office at the following address:

U.S. Patent and Trademark Office
2021 Jefferson Davis Hwy.
Arlington, VA 20231
(703) 557-3158

Activity: Company Name

Make a list of all the words that describe your company. Go to the public library and look at all the area phone books to assist you with the process. As you create a name you like, check the local phone books to see if another business exists by that name. Next, take a list of at least ten possible names and discuss them with the key people in your life. Interview other people, describe your company and then ask them which name from your list of ten fits best.

Location

You need to consider many factors when selecting a location for your business. The following five factors are key to your process of choosing a business location.

- Type of Business — Are your competitors in office or retail space? In this type of business, do your customers come to you or do you go to the customers?

- Cost — Can you afford office space or could you just operate out of your home until you have some income? Many of the largest companies in the country started out home based. Home-based business is a growing trend. More and more people are eliminating their commute to work from the comfort of their home.

- Image — What type of image do you want or need to project. If you want a more upscale look you will need to spend more on office space. Evaluate whether this increase in cost is warranted. After all, the way your office looks isn't going to recruit new distributors or sell products.
- Space Requirements — Will you have employees? Do you need room for equipment? How much room will you need at projected growth for the year?
- Zoning — Zoning is a particular concern for home-based businesses. Some areas are not zoned for home-based businesses or have restrictions on the activities. Before starting a business from your home, check on the zoning.

The remainder of this section discusses the two types of locations you will be considering as a network marketer, a home-based business, or a business with an office outside your home.

Home Based

An increasing number of people are starting home-based businesses. CNN reports that a home-based business is started every 60 seconds in the U.S. Why this phenomenon?

A number of reasons explain why Americans are turning to home-based business. Corporate downsizing has forced many middle- and upper-level managers out of a shrinking job market. These former executives can't find jobs that equal their previous incomes, so they start home-based businesses. Forced early retirement has also created a large number of pre-retirement entrepreneurs who operate from their home. In her best selling book, *The Popcorn Report*[1], Faith Popcorn refers to a baby boomer trend called "cashing out." The baby boomer generation is leaving the high stress corporate world to start small businesses. Many of these new small businesses are home based, which allows baby boomer entrepreneurs to be closer to their kids and to eliminate commuting. Network marketing creates a perfect opportunity for people to start a low risk, home-based business.

---

[1] *The Popcorn Report*, Faith Popcorn, (New York: Doubleday Currency, 1991), p. 50.

Whatever your reason for considering a home-based business, you need to understand the pitfalls. First, by having a business in your home, you can never leave work. Work will always be there staring you in the face. Many people can't deal with the stress working at home creates. Some become workaholics, jeopardizing their relationship with their family For some, the opposite occurs — distractions keep people from doing their work. House or yard work, television, children, pets, and the telephone can keep you from accomplishing what you need to in order to make your business successful. Finally, some people are bothered by the isolation of working at home. Many home-based entrepreneurs can't handle the quiet and lack of other people, so they move to an office where there is more hustle and bustle.

If you can avoid the pitfalls and treat your home-based business like a big business, you can enjoy the benefits.

- No commute — You can reduce gas expenditures and the wear and tear on your car. Because you don't have to spend time driving to and from work, you can spend more time at productive work.
- Flexible schedule — You can work whenever you want. You can play with your kids in the afternoon and then work late at night or early in the morning. If you have to drive to an office, you cannot schedule your work and personal life as conveniently.
- Accessibility — You are more accessible to your family. If friends or family have an emergency, you are available to help. Many people find that when they work out of an office, they feel isolated from their family. Working at home can change that.
- Reduced costs — You pay no additional rent, utilities, signage costs, or maintenance fees to have your office at home. If you are operating on a tight budget, a home-based office can help you get the business started and keep it going.

Having a home-based business can be the best thing that every happened to your career or it can become a nightmare. Here are some suggestions that will help you create a workable situation.

First, if possible, set up your office in a separate room or part of the house. A spare bedroom or den makes a good office. Make sure that the room has a door that can be shut and, if needed, locked. It is best if the entire room is dedicated to your business so that you can minimize distractions.

Second, set up a comfortable and professional workspace. Necessary equipment and furniture include a desk or computer work station, a comfortable chair that rolls, a bookcase, a computer, printer, fax, and copier. Because you will be working alone most of the time, you may want to hang motivational posters on the walls and play tapes as you work. If you have enough room, set up space where you can hold small meetings. You need room for a few chairs and a white board on one wall. If you use video tapes in your presentation, you will also need a TV and VCR.

Next, set up the office rules for the rest of the family. Let them know that when the door is closed, you are at work. Some home-based entrepreneurs make up a sign that indicates they are working and are not to be disturbed. This sign can be placed on the door during times when you need to concentrate.

Lighting is important to your comfort. Operating a business can be depressing enough without sitting in a dimly lit dungeon. Natural light is the best, so try to set up your office in a room that has a window or skylight. If natural light is not possible, set up lamps so that you have light coming from every corner and from above.

Generally, the biggest concern about a home office is the degree of professionalism you can achieve there. Set up your office in a professional manner and adopt a professional attitude. Be proud of your office and project your pride to people who might meet you there. You will probably find most visitors envious of your situation.

Office Outside the Home

Having an office outside the home has its advantages and disadvantages also. You should consider these carefully before making the decision to locate in an outside office. Some advantages to an office outside the home include:

- Credibility — A business office has a higher level of credibility than a home-based office. Many people think that if you have an office, you are a real business. It inspires confidence in your business.

Network marketing already has a credibility problem. You may find that having an office outside the home is particularly important for your network marketing business.

- Comfort — An office outside the home may be more socially comfortable for you and your clients. Many businesswomen in particular feel uncomfortable inviting customers or prospects, people who may be strangers, into their home. They may feel uncomfortable as well.

- Convenience — Depending on where your house is located, an office in a business district may be more convenient for your customers. Consider this issue seriously if most of your customers will be coming to you.

- Separation — An office outside the home allows you to separate home and business. When you leave the office, it is easier to leave your business behind, and you don't have to worry about family interruptions or home distractions.

While having an office outside the home may carry some advantages that are important to you, you also need to consider the disadvantages.

- Cost — The cost of having an office outside the home is probably the biggest disadvantage. You either have to rent or buy an office and pay higher start-up costs and higher monthly expenses. You may also have to pay for utilities and cleaning. If you are short on start-up cash but have determined that you need an office away from the home, find a location where you can negotiate a twelve month lease with the first two or three months payable at the end of the lease. This arrangement allows you to pay no rent for the first two or three months, but the lease would extend for 14 or 15 months, instead of just 12.

- Daycare Costs — While this is not a concern to all of you, it is to some. Many entrepreneurs with children are able to keep their children home while working in their home office. With the high cost of daycare these days, saving on this costly monthly expense is a definite bonus to a home office

- The Commute — You want to locate an office that is convenient to your clients or customers, not to you. One of the biggest mistakes an entrepreneur can make, in selecting location, is to rent an office close to home. However, because the office is convenient to your customers, it may be far away from home and require a stressful daily commute.

- Duplication — Network marketing is a business of duplication. How many of the distributors you sponsor will have the money to duplicate your office situation? A home office is much easier to duplicate. You don't want to scare away potential distributors by giving them the idea that they need to pay for an outside office as you do.

A great option to the stand alone office is an executive or office suite. These are large office spaces that have been sub-divided into small one- or two-person offices. They generally offer reception and telephone answering services, copier and fax use, and possibly secretarial services. These offices are more expensive per square foot, but generally less expensive per month because they are smaller than stand alone offices. Plus, you have available services and equipment you would otherwise have to purchase yourself. You can find executive suites in many of the large office buildings in your city. Some of the executive suites offer space for rent on a need basis for an hourly fee. You could meet prospects or new distributors at this type of office, allowing you to create a better image at the meeting, or to meet people for the first time at an outside office rather than have strangers into your home.

You also might consider setting up your own mini-suite by securing a space and sharing it with a number of other distributors in your company. These may be your sponsor, people you recruit, or just other distributors in the area. If you all contribute to the cost of the space, furniture, office equipment, and advertising, it will be much cheaper.

Activity: Location

Talk with at least two people who operate their business from home and two that use an office outside the home. Ask for their recommendation. Next, decide whether you will operate from home or outside the home. If you will start home based, begin preparing the space. If you will operate outside the home, call several local property managers and have them help you locate an appropriate office space. Discuss the idea of sharing space with your sponsor and upline leader.

Licensing

Every state has different requirements regarding the licensing of a new business. In most states you will need a local business license, and some require a state license also. Certain industries require special licenses or permits. Network marketing is not one of those industries. However, as an example, if you were marketing life insurance products, you will need a special license. Contact the department of business licensing in your state, or consult your state's edition of The Oasis Press' *Starting and Operating a Business* series for more information on the licensing requirements in your state.

Taxes

Every business pays taxes to the federal government, the IRS. C corporations pay the tax directly, whereas in a sole proprietorship, partnership, or subchapter S corporation, the income passes through to the individual owner(s) and is taxed as personal income. No tax is withheld, so you will need to set up a system in which the appropriate amount from each check is deposited into a separate account and paid to the IRS quarterly.

Local taxes differ in each state, so check with the state department of revenue to see what taxes you must pay to the state, county, or city, or check your state's edition of The Oasis Press' *Starting and Operating a Business* series.

Lastly, if you have employees, you will need to pay payroll taxes. Have your employees complete a W-4 form and withhold a certain amount of taxes from each check. Escrow this money in a separate bank account and send it to the IRS. At the end of each year, you issue a W-2 form to each employee, showing them total earnings and the amount you withheld.

If, on the other hand, you choose to use independent contractors or sub-contractors for any extra labor or services you need performed, the tax situation is different. If you pay an independent contractor more than $600 in a year, you must issue them an IRS form 1099 showing their earnings.

As a network marketer, all of the distributors you recruit are independent contractors. They own their own business and are not considered to be employees. This means that they too will need to be licensed and pay taxes on the money they earn. If your network marketing company pays distributors directly, they will send the 1099 forms directly to your distributors. On the other hand, if you pay your distributors bonuses, you will need to issue the 1099s. Also, as your network grows, you may want to hire an assistant, secretary, or telemarketer. You will need to deal with these people as employees.

You must mail both the W-2 and 1099 to the appropriate person by January 31. Your accountant will be of great assistance in helping you understand and accomplish this task.

Telephone

Now that you have your office location and licensing, it is time to arrange for telephones. If you do some advance planning setting up your telephone system, you can save thousands of dollars.

You can purchase many different types of phones — single line, two-line, key system, and PBX are the primary types. If you are starting a one-person office and plan to stay that way for at least a year, go to your local electronics supply store and purchase a high quality, two-line telephone with speakerphone, speed dial, and a hold button. The cost should be under $100. The speakerphone can be a very useful tool, particularly in the beginning of your network marketing career. Your sponsor or upline leader can give a presentation or part of a presentation over the speakerphone. The speakerphone is useful for training new distributors as well.

On the other hand, if you are planning to hire a number of people, determine how many people you will have at start-up, how many in one year, and how many in three years. Then contact a number of telephone equipment vendors and find one that has the knowledge to help you design a system to meet your needs.

Deciding what type of telephone service you will purchase can be complicated. When you order a telephone line, you may be offered services such as call waiting, three-way calling, and call forwarding. If you are only using one line, purchase the call waiting service; it is like having two lines for about $2 per month. Three-way calling is like conference calling. You can connect two other people with yourself for a conference call. You will need this so that you can three-way call prospective distributors with your sponsor and network distributors. Call forwarding allows you to forward your business line to another number, such as a cellular phone, voice mail, home phone, or another business location. All of these services can be helpful and tend to be very inexpensive.

As a network marketer, you will be making frequent long-distance calls, so you need to choose a long-distance carrier you think provides competitive rates. Several carriers are vying for business customers, so you shouldn't have trouble getting a good deal. In fact, there are a number of network marketing companies that offer long distance services and pre-programmed phone cards.

You also need to choose between voice mail, an answering service, or an answering machine for answering your telephone when you are unavailable to take calls. Each has advantages and disadvantages.

Voice mail is probably the most efficient way to have your telephone answered when you are not available. It allows you to record a message in your own voice, which can be changed daily or throughout the day. Most voice mail systems allow you to retrieve messages from any touch tone phone and in some cases can be connected with a pager, so you know instantly about messages. Voice mail sounds better than an answering machine and allows you to retrieve messages more easily, but costs more. Chapter 5 discusses some ways you can use independent voice mail boxes for prospecting. You can also rent voice mail boxes from your telephone company or from independent companies. Look in the Yellow Pages under Voice Mail, Telephone — Voice Mail, or Telephone — Answering.

Answering services offer you the professional touch of a live person answering your phone. When a live person answers your phone, your business looks bigger because you appear to have a secretary or receptionist. Also, some people respond better to a live rather than a recorded voice. However, using an answering service often carries a high cost, and sometimes the people who answer your phone aren't as professional as you would like. To locate an answering service, look in the Yellow Pages under Answering Service or Telephone — Answering Service.

The good, old answering machine has the highest upfront cost, but the lowest usage cost. The new, high-tech, digital machines can cost as much as $200 and have many of the same features as voice mail. Avoid the older, tape machines as they can cause you many headaches — lost messages, bad tapes, and messages that can't be retrieved away from the office. The only real advantage to an answering machine is that you own the equipment and have no monthly service charges.

In today's high tech society, nearly everyone has a cellular phone. Should you have one? If your business requires that you travel in the car for a large part of your work day, or if it is critical that people reach you when you are out of the office, then you should probably have a cellular phone. The major cost is the service. In most areas you can get phones for free or at a very low cost if you sign up on a guaranteed program, which usually lasts for a full year. If you are going to use the cellular phone often, try to get a monthly service package that includes the estimated number of minutes you will use. These offer cheaper per minute rates and will save you money.

If you just need to receive messages promptly, a pager might be a better answer than a cellular phone. The cost is much lower.

Banking

As you begin your business, the only part your bank will play is to provide your business checking account. As a start-up business, your odds of getting a loan are very slim unless you take out a personal line of credit based on collateral. However, starting a relationship with your bank and its loan officers now can benefit you in the future.

When you select a bank, try to find one that caters to small businesses. Your local banks are more likely candidates than the big national or regional banks. Take the time to interview a banker about the services that are offered to small businesses. You will want to find a bank that offers business checking at the lowest rates, short-term loans, and safety deposit boxes. Most banks have these services, so your primary concerns will be fees and your comfort level with the people. Investigate also the proximity of the bank to your office and the number of branches. Instead of a bank you may want to consider a credit union. They are quite often more amiable to small businesses. Particularly when it comes to loans and lines of credit.

Once you have selected a financial institution, schedule a meeting with whomever is responsible for lending money to small businesses. The purpose of the meeting is not to borrow money, but rather to introduce yourself and your business, and to establish a relationship. Take along a copy of your business plan and discuss your anticipated future financial needs. Find out what the financial institution requires from a small business owner to apply for a loan. Ask for hints on things you might do to increase your odds of getting a loan later on when you need some additional funding.

Bookkeeping

As a small business owner, you have two choices. You can choose to handle the bookkeeping and accounting tasks yourself, or you can assign them to a full-time bookkeeping or accounting firm.

Every new business owner should handle his or her own bookkeeping for at least six months so that they have a better understanding of the procedures. Doing your own bookkeeping in the beginning will help you work with a bookkeeper or accountant in the future. Unless you are a trained accountant and insist on a complicated double entry system, keep your bookkeeping system very simple. Consult The Oasis Press' *Bottom Line Basics* for a complete analysis of accounting and financial management for small businesses.

Depending on which parent company you represent, you may receive computer printouts that show your network of distributors and their volumes. If your company has a program for the retail customers to order directly from the parent company, then you may also receive a printout showing their activity. Keep two files with these reports for reference at tax time.

Why do you need to keep records? An effective small business book-keeping and accounting system should have a number of objectives, including:

- To provide tax records, as required by law;
- To give an accurate picture of operating results;
- To help you with forecasting and budgeting;
- To provide financial statements for obtaining financing;
- To facilitate the prompt and accurate filing of tax returns; and
- To reveal employee fraud, theft, waste, or errors.

A basic accounting system will include the following records:

- Cash — Shows all receipts and disbursements of cash to help you determine current and forecast future cash flow.
- Accounts Receivable — Shows all customers who owe you money, a record of payments, and your balance. Network marketing is a cash business. When you sell products you receive cash at the time of the order, so you should never have any accounts receivables.
- Accounts Payable — Shows the creditors to whom you owe money and the amount.
- Inventory — Applicable if you maintain and sell products; shows the stock levels and helps with computation of stock turnover ratios.
- Payroll — Applicable if you have employees; shows the total payments to employees and provides the information necessary to pay various payroll taxes.

If your business is a simple cash business with no employees, you can buy simple accounting systems at any office supply store. If you would like a little more detail on how to combine your checkbook and bookkeeping system, you can find many excellent software systems, including The Oasis' Press Financial Templates.

After you have handled your own books for about six months, or, if at this point you do not feel capable of handling the accounting, start interviewing bookkeeping services. Do not go with the cheapest, but rather find a professional service with at least five years of experience with small businesses. Use a bookkeeping service rather than an accountant for your day-to-day books because it is less costly. You will still need the accountant for taxes and questions regarding more complicated issues.

A bookkeeping service will take all of your weekly receipts and disbursement data and enter it into a computer accounting system. They will generate statements so that you can get an overall view of your financial situation. After you have used the service for a number of months, you can begin comparing the monthly statements to help you with forecasting and budgeting.

You should save all the statements from the bookkeeping service and give them to your accountant for quarterly or annual taxes. Since the bookkeeping service is doing all the daily entries and consolidations, your accountant will have minimal work, so your total accounting costs should be small.

Poor recordkeeping is one of the most common reasons for business failure, so make sure you either develop and keep a good set of books, or hire a service to do so.

Insurance

Insurance is something almost every business owner buys and hopes they never need. Insurance can be confusing, so new business owners often procrastinate in the purchase. You need to get past the confusion and mystique.

You should purchase insurance to protect against major financial loss. The first thing you need to do is identify the business risks you need covered by insurance — loss of property, loss of life, financial loss due to liability, financial loss due to interruption of your business, employee theft, burglary, or robbery. Once you have identified the risks, you can contact an insurance agent to investigate the appropriate insurance.

The best way to select an agent is to ask other businesspeople whom they use. Get some recommendations and then interview the agents over the phone. Agents who have earned the Chartered Life Underwriter (CLU) designation, as a rule, will be more experienced and better able to fill your needs. You may find that you have to work with both a CLU and a property and casualty agent to get the best coverage. In any case, find people whom you like and who have experience working with small businesses. A good agent will help you obtain the best coverage for the lowest possible cost.

The types of insurance small businesses most commonly need include:

- Property Insurance — Covers your building, equipment, and inventory.
- Liability Insurance — Protects you against financial loss due to customer or employee claims of bodily or monetary injury, resulting in a lawsuit.
- Business Interruption Insurance — Provides protection against loss of income due to an unexpected temporary shutdown, such as a shutdown due to fire or fire-related damage.
- Keyperson Insurance — Provides protection against potential loss of revenue due to the death of a key individual in your business, usually a partner. You can also use this type of insurance in community property states to settle a partnership conflict with the family after a partner has died; the family receives the proceeds from the policy in exchange for the remaining share of ownership and the right to continue the business.

Check with your company to see if they carry a group liability policy that covers you. Evaluate the limitations and discuss these with your agent. Also, research any other group policies that the company offers. For helpful strategies on buying insurance and managing risk, consult The Oasis Press' *The Buyer's Guide to Business Insurance.*

It is essential that you insure any aspect of your business that is critical to success, whether it be equipment, inventory, or a key person. Do not overlook this area. One loss could be catastrophic!

Professional Advisers

As you start your new business, you will quickly discover that everyone in your life is an expert adviser. Many have never operated a business, but they sure know what you should do.

You need some professional advisers to help make the important decisions. This group could consist of family members, friends, and business associates. These advisers will not be payed, so they need to be people who are sincerely interested in your well-being and success. They should also be people who have a variety of business experiences. The role of an adviser is to:

- Help with brainstorming new ideas;
- Evaluate and give input on your business plan;
- Verify financial data;
- Provide assistance with solutions to difficult problems;
- Supply expertise where it is missing;
- Help with leads for business and financing; and
- Objectively evaluate the performance of the business.

If you are able, set up a board of advisers that meets at least twice a year. Take them to lunch and have an established agenda of items you would like to discuss. Of course, you can contact the advisers individually more often. These people should have no vested interest and nothing to lose by giving you honest input. Do not put your banker, accountant, attorney, financial planner, or bookkeeper on the board. Use your advisers when you need them, but don't abuse them. Keep in mind that they have other lives. On the other hand, if you don't use them, they will disappear. Don't create a board of advisers just for show; your advisers should actively assist you with the growth of your company.

You also want a second type of advisory group that includes your banker, accountant, attorney, financial planner, and bookkeeper. Select these people carefully. They will be very influential in the success of your business.

Marketing Materials

Choosing marketing materials is an area sorely neglected in most small businesses. At the start-up stage, a small business owner usually does one of two things — the owner either buys the cheapest basic business card, letterhead, and envelope package he or she can find, or the owner gets hooked by an agency to create incredibly beautiful, but expensive and ineffective materials. Your initial marketing materials should fall somewhere in between. Check with your parent company — many network marketing companies offer very attractive business cards, color brochures, and direct mailers for very little money. If your network marketing company does not have marketing materials that suit your needs, you may need to create your own.

Prior to actually creating any materials, work with a graphic designer to create a logo for your company, a symbol that represents your company. Find a designer who specializes in corporate-type logos. Ask to see examples and select someone who has a style you like. A professional designer will develop three to seven designs, fine-tune one, and provide you a camera-ready version for under $1,000. Take your time and shop around. Your logo is a very important part of your image.

Now that you have a logo, you can begin creating materials. For business cards, letterhead, envelopes, thank-you notes, note pads, and mailing labels, use a desktop publisher. A good one will take your logo and place it into a basic design and then provide you with camera-ready copy that you can take to a printer.

If you are designing a brochure, catalog, or direct mail piece, have your graphic designer assist. They have been professionally trained to develop these very important marketing pieces. As you develop these materials, keep in mind that most designers are not marketers, they are designers. Their primary concern is the way the piece looks. Your top concern is the effectiveness of the piece. Work with the designer to accomplish both.

The key marketing materials you want to develop and have printed at this early stage include:

- Business card — They will sell for you after you are gone, and they should extend a professional image and remind the prospect of what you do. You will be giving cards to every prospect, so keep that in mind when ordering quantities.
- Letterhead and envelopes — They should match your business card and remain basic and traditional.

- Brochure — A brochure tells your story, explains your product or service, gives the benefits for purchasing your product or using your service, and compels them to do business with you. It may also explain the concept of network marketing and promote the benefits of being a distributor.

- Thank-you note — Thank-you notes are used to thank prospects, customers, and suppliers. You want them to be in the same style as your business cards, letterhead, and envelopes. A 5½" x 8½" card with your logo on the front, folded and placed in an A2 envelope is best. You can also find several executive greeting cards for sale, including those produced be Execards, a division of PSI Research.

- Presentation folder — The folder should have your logo on the outside, use company colors, and have two pockets inside for proposals or company documents and slots for your business card. This is great to give a prospect who needs to consult with a spouse or potential partner.

- Catalog — Catalogs come in various sizes, include photos or line drawings, use one or two color or full color. Decide what works best for you. A catalog is a good tool if you sell a large line of products. These are generally supplied by the network marketing company at very reasonable prices.

- Direct mailer — Direct mailers are promotional pieces designed specifically for mailings and are available in various sizes and designs. Its primary focus should be to move the prospect to action — to order, call, or stop by your store. Direct mail is a great way to accomplish more prospecting in less time.

The uses of these marketing materials are covered in greater detail in Chapter 4: Retailing and Chapter 5: Prospecting. Refer to these chapters prior to any final decisions.

Invest just enough money in your marketing materials to get the image you want, but not too much image. Also, check with your company to find out what marketing materials it provides. Usually, the company purchases marketing materials in large quantities, so you can get a very good price for high quality materials.

Activity: Logo

Contact your network marketing company to determine what marketing materials they have available. Plan the development of anything they don't have.

Product Knowledge

As you will discover, retailing gives your business its long-term strength. To retail your products, you must gain the necessary knowledge. The best way to learn about your products is to use them yourself and see what they do for you. The premise behind network marketing is that if you are excited about something, you will tell others about it. How can you be excited about your products if you have never used them?

Check with your company to see what other methods of product training it offers. They may provide training seminars or workshops, video or audio tapes, and written materials. You may also want to do some outside research. For example, if you are marketing nutritional products, you should research the nutrition market to see how your products rate among competitors. Get input from people who are not in your business. Give or sell samples of your products to some of your friends and family for their input.

Keep in mind that to be a successful network marketer, you do not need to be a product expert. No advanced degrees in chemistry, biology, or dermatology are necessary. Just use the products, study the training materials, get some outside input, and talk about those products that really excite you.

Compensation Plan

Most people come into the business side of network marketing because of the potential to create financial and time freedom. You can acquire financial and time freedom because of the unique compensation plans you will find in network marketing. To tell people how they can make money with your company, you need to have a flawless understanding of the compensation plan.

Most network marketing companies include in their distributor kit a good description of their compensation plan. Study this and write down any questions. Set an appointment with your sponsor or upline leader to discuss and clarify the compensation plan. Once you understand the plan, you can more easily describe how your prospective distributor can make money. Chapter 1 describes four different types of compensation plans commonly used by network marketing companies.

After you have done some of this preliminary work to prepare yourself and your new company for business, you are ready to start talking to people about the products and opportunity. If you are like most new network marketers, you are excited and scared to death. What do you say? What if they ask a question you can't answer? Don't let yourself become paralyzed by your fears. Turn to Chapter 2 and reread what success principles you identified. Go talk to people, and think of each presentation as practice. Each time you talk with someone, you are practicing.

Many new network marketers fail because they never get started. Don't let your analysis of your business create paralysis. The only way you can fail in this business is to quit.

Chapter 4

Retailing

Retailing is the Crux of Network Marketing

Too many network marketers have been enticed into this industry by the myth that retailing products is not necessary. Don't be misled — retailing is the crux of this business. Without the movement of products from the company to the consumer through distributors, no one makes any money. It is true that the big money is in building a large network, but if you do not sell products, your bonuses will be much lower.

You need to retail your products for two main reasons.

- Retail sales will result in immediate income, which creates excitement and long-term commitment.
- The distributors you recruit will duplicate your efforts. If you are a good retailer, they will be also.

You need to stress to your new distributors the importance of building a good retail base prior to a major push on sponsoring. Retailing not only brings money into your network, but it also helps you find new distributors. Distributors often start as retail buyers, then become wholesale buyers, then retailers, and eventually are business builders. Called the bottom up approach to network marketing, your primary concentration is on retailing. When people who purchase your product get excited about the results, some will want to become distributors, and that is how you build a network. If you build your business in this manner, you will rely on referrals. Every time you talk with someone about your products, ask who they know that might like to look at the products. Keep track of who gives you referrals so that, as you develop new customers, you can go back to the people who gave you referrals and show them how they can make some money.

For example, if you approach Mary and introduce her to your products, and she enjoys and benefits from them, she may refer you to Tom, John, and Sue. You contact each of them, and they all purchase some products. You now go back to Mary and discuss the amount of money she could have made. Then let her know that if she signs on as a distributor and commits to working the program, at least part-time, you will give her Tom, John, and Sue as customers.

Use the Products

Network marketing is nothing more than sharing a product, service, or concept with people. How could you possibly share the benefits of your products without using them? The first key to success in network marketing is to become a product of the products. You need to become your own best customer. Use all of your products, so that you can share first hand experience with them. Talk about the taste or texture, share why you like it or what it did for you. Until potential customers actually try your product, you have to paint a picture with words, full of enough graphic detail and emotion to move them to action.

In network marketing, you don't have to be a product expert, but you do need to have a good understanding of what your products are and the benefits they provide. Using the products is the best way to gain product knowledge. Most likely your company also provides literature that lists the ingredients, features, and benefits of your products. Check your distributor manual for product information too.

Another great way to get product knowledge is to talk with other people who have used the products. Talk with other distributors and customers. Find out which products they have used and what they liked and disliked. Ask them how they feel about the price. As you are gathering this information, make up a benefits worksheet that shows each product and the derived benefits. Make up a list of the most common product questions you hear. Work with your sponsor or upline leader to develop effective answers to these questions. Then start sharing the products with people.

Share Your Products with Others

Product sales in network marketing happen naturally. Somewhere in a conversation with friends, co-workers, family, business associates, or parents, a statement will be made that naturally leads to a conversation about your products. For example, if you market a line of nutritional products, and someone mentions that they just don't seem to have as much energy any more, you have a great opening to begin talking about your products. If you sell skin care products, someone may mention how old they are starting to look or how dry their skin has been lately. If you market alarm systems, someone may comment about a house near them that was burglarized. If you stay aware, you will find many opportunities to talk about your products, but only if you have used your products and have confidence that they will do what they are supposed to.

Sampling

If your company offers samples or you can create them yourself, giving away samples is an excellent way to introduce people to your products. What better way to show customers your product's quality and benefits than to have them actually use the products. Skin care companies have been using this method for years. As you walk through a department store, you find dozens of samples you can try or free makeover offers because the companies know that you will like the way their product feels and want to purchase some. You become emotionally committed, even before you hear the price.

One network marketing skin care company uses a party approach to share samples. They invite several people over for a skin care clinic. The leader educates the potential customers while allowing them to try some of the products. After the clinic, which lasts about an hour, the leader answers questions and takes orders. An average clinic with four or five people can generate $100 to $500 in retail sales.

Another company that markets weight management products uses a similar approach. Distributors conduct weight management seminars to educate people about why traditional, low calorie diets don't work and how their program does. Again, the leader answers questions and takes orders. Distributors often average $50 in sales per person attending.

A popular sampler method for skin care products is the pamper basket. The distributor fills a wicker basket full of products, instructions for use, an opportunity video or audio, and a catalog. The potential customer gets to use the products, watch the video, and read the catalog for two or three days. Distributors tend to enjoy an average of $40 in sales per basket. This method is so successful because the potential customer gets to use the actual size products, can examine the ingredients carefully, and can use the products in the comfort of their own home without any perceived sales pressure.

A version of sampling used by network marketing distributors who sell hardware, such as water filters or alarm systems, is the trial approach. Distributors get a prospect to commit to trying the product for a few days to a few weeks. Salespeople call this the puppy dog approach. Once you have that cute little puppy in your arms, it's hard to give it back. Once you have that product in your house or car, it's easier to buy it than give it back.

Sampling can be an effective way to market your products. It can also be expensive. Follow-up is very important. Don't assume that your products are so good that they will sell themselves. No product is that good. You need to call the people back and see how they liked the samples. Chances are good they will not even have tried them yet, but your call will be a good reminder.

Audio and Video Presentations

Testimonials can be tremendously powerful when marketing products. Potential buyers like to know that other people have purchased and like the products. Most network marketing companies have audio or video tapes with product information and testimonials. A short audio tape is a great way to introduce the products.

Some products are more visually oriented or require visual directions. In this case, video is the better media. You can leverage your retailing by using the video as a salesperson.

You can mail video and audio tapes, allowing you to expand your distribution to other cities, states, or even countries. Audio or video tapes are a mobile, flexible, yet powerful means of giving a product presentation.

Brochures and Catalogs

Home shopping has experienced a dramatic increase in the last five years. More Americans are eliminating the frustration of parking and fighting the crowds at the mall to instead purchase products via mail order catalogs and television shopping. If your company offers a drop ship program, shipping the products directly to the customer, that allows customers to call and order using your distributor number, then you too can participate in this marketing phenomenon.

The prospects are everywhere. Start with all the people you know outside your immediate geographic area. If you want to expand, you can purchase, actually lease, mailing lists of people who are already avid home shoppers. You can even identify people who regularly purchase your type of products, whether nutritional supplements, cleaning supplies, or skin care. Mail a catalog with a personalized letter or note instructing customers how to order and why your products are so much better.

Brochures are more focused, so they can be used for groups of people who are likely to have interest in a particular product. You can mail brochures separately or with a catalog.

Education

If your product does something good for people, but they are not educated in that area you could offer educational seminars. For example, you could hold seminars called Live Longer and Healthier, Getting Older — Looking Younger, The Truth About Your Water and Air, depending on what product you sell. You can offer these seminars to schools, large corporations, real estate or insurance offices, government entities, and health clubs.

If you have the ability and enjoy speaking to groups of people, this concept can be very powerful. Develop a short seminar, 30 to 45 minutes long, on a subject relating to your product line. Make sure that it contains useful information, rather than just a promotion for your products. However, you are there to generate business, so make sure the information causes listeners to consider buying your product.

Give a free information pack containing literature and samples to everyone who gives you a business card or completes a small information sheet. Follow-up with these people to get input on your talk and the literature they received.

Fund Raising

One great way to build your retail sales volume is to get non-profit groups to promote your products as a fund raiser. You will keep part of the profit and they get the rest.

Schools, churches, and other non-profit groups are always looking for ways to raise funds. Talk with the fund raising coordinator about your products and how they might work for their organization. Again, if your company offers a program in which the customer can order directly and have the product drop shipped, you can show the coordinator a powerful fund raiser. Members can just pass out catalogs and do a little suggestive selling, without inventory hassles, money processing, recordkeeping, or product delivery. These sales will contribute to your retail profits and the non-profit will make money too. Plus, if they are innovative and participate in the network building side, they can create a perpetual income stream that may eliminate the need for future fund raisers.

For example, a church in Texas is funded entirely through a network marketing program. It began promoting products and building a network in the late 1980s and now has a residual income of more than $40,000 per month. Many of the congregation, who participated in the program, also received financial benefit.

Lead Box

You have probably seen lead boxes in restaurants or stores, advertising free health club memberships or time share vacations. Lead boxes are simply boxes with an advertisement designed to stimulate people to put their name, address, and phone number in the box. Contests tend to be most successful in eliciting responses. If you decide to run a contest, choose something you can give away that has high perceived value, but that doesn't cost you very much.

If you use the lead box method to generate leads on potential customers, begin by making two or three boxes, making sure to spend enough money to make them look professional. If you don't want to take the time to make them, contact office products retailers in your area to see if they have something similar. You may need to contact a box manufacturer.

Next, take your box and go to your favorite restaurant. Ask to speak with the manager. Tell the manager that you are a regular customer and refer a lot of business to the restaurant — this is a nice compliment and will warm the manager up to you. Continue by saying that you are currently expanding your business and would appreciate his or her help by allowing you to place the lead box in the lobby or restroom.

Set up two or three and check them each week. Take the leads and either call to see if they have any interest in your products or opportunity or mail them an information pack. If you mail information, follow-up with a phone call within 72 hours.

Coupons

Coupons are a great way to sell products, however, distribution is usually a problem. Cost can be another concern. One way to minimize both would be to create a cooperative coupon. You could go out and talk with local merchants, such as a video store, restaurant, hair or tanning salon, to see if they would be interested in splitting the cost of a cooperative coupon. A cooperative coupon is usually made out of a standard half sheet of paper, 5½" x 8½", containing four different coupons, one of which would be a promotion for your products. You arrange for the design, printing, and distribution, and the other advertisers pay three-fourths of the cost. Your costs remain low, and you have three places in which to distribute your coupons. You also have an opportunity to prospect the other three business owners.

You will also find cooperative coupon mailing services in almost every town. Look in the Yellow Pages under Advertising — Cooperative or Coupon. The cooperative coupon mailing service designs and prints the coupon for you, and then mails yours along with a number of others to at least 10,000 homes. The cost is typically around $400, or $.04 per household. Certain products, such as weight loss programs, household cleaners, and wrinkle creams tend to sell well through cooperative coupons.

Telemarketing

If you like to talk with people on the phone, telemarketing may be a good retail avenue for you. Develop a short product-oriented script. Surveys work well in telemarketing. You can ask questions about health and then pitch your nutrition product, about the environment to pitch your air or water filters or environmentally safe cleaners, about home security to sell alarm systems, or about aging for skin care products. Your script should begin by introducing you and your company. Second, give the purpose for your call, which should create some interest. Third, ask a question to test customers' interest level. Finally, gain commitment from the customer to watch a video, listen to an audio, look at your catalog, try some samples, attend a seminar or clinic, accept a product trial, or purchase a sample pack. If they are not interested, just thank them for their time. Network marketing does not require pushy sales. However, always try to ask for referrals, and you might even throw in a plug for the opportunity to network market, "You wouldn't happen to know anyone who could use an extra $1,000 a month, would you?"

Telemarketing is purely a numbers game. Most people will not be interested, some will be rude, and others will just hang up on you. Be mentally prepared to do battle. Telemarketers' favorite saying is "Some will, some won't, so what, next!"

If you are going to commit to telemarketing as a way to market your products, schedule a time every day to call, and set a minimum number of calls you will make. Memorize and internalize your script so that it sounds natural. Stay relaxed, speak slowly but with enthusiasm, and, as always in network marketing, smile and have fun.

Walking and Talking

Take some of your samples and head for the mall, not to shop, but to prospect. Strike up conversations with other patrons or with sales clerks. Give people samples of your product and get their names and phone numbers so you can get their input after they try the product.

You can go just about anywhere there are people to talk and hand out samples. Just make sure you get business cards or at least names and phone numbers so you can follow-up.

Partner Program

If you are using the clinic or home party approach, a partner program is an excellent way to increase business. When you have a customer who has purchased a certain amount of your products, you set the amount, they can become a partner. They arrange the next clinic or party, and you give them a percentage of the retail sales in the form of a gift certificate redeemable for your products. That way they can get their own products free by helping you.

When you have someone at a clinic or party who purchases the necessary amount of products, they too can become a partner. Can you see how you could create a real chain effect? Partnering can be a very effective program.

Tradeshows

Check with your company to see if you can participate in tradeshows. Some network marketing companies will not allow you to participate in tradeshows, because they feel it gives unfair advantage to those distributors who have more money. If so, call the chamber of commerce for a list of the tradeshows in your area. Also, you might want to check on swap meets. Many of the old drive-in theaters have been converted. Booth space is cheap and particularly on weekends you can get quite a bit of exposure for very little money.

If you market nutritional products, check with the health clubs and hospitals to see if they have any health or fitness fairs scheduled. Let them know that you would be interested in participating. Home shows are great for water filters, home cleaning products, and alarm systems. Auto shows are perfect for car alarm systems.

For optimal success at a tradeshow, set up some kind of activity in which prospects can participate. An activity attracts customers to the booth and keeps them there longer. Games and contests are almost always successful. Sampling keeps customers at the booth and allows them to try your product. Make sure you have inexpensive information you can give to everyone, and a more expensive, detailed information pack you give only to people who show a high level of interest.

If you don't have enough money for the booth, try sharing it with your upline, downline, or other local distributors. If that doesn't work, just attend the tradeshow and talk with vendors. Pick up business cards and get names and numbers for later contact.

Activity: Retailing

Pick out two or three methods you will use and begin retailing the products. Set a goal for ten new customers by a certain date.

Price Objections

One of the advantages of network marketing is that the number of middlepeople have been reduced, which cuts costs. Generally, network marketing companies will put these savings into higher quality ingredients. What you end up with is a product that is far superior to anything on the market and priced slightly higher than the market. In some cases, the product is so radically different that it costs much more than the average product of its type. In these cases, you may hear price objections. Here are some ideas for handling them.

First, throughout your contact with a prospect, constantly talk value. Quite often, if you build enough value in a higher priced product, you won't get the price objections. Talk about higher quality and more expensive ingredients in your product that produce better results. Talk personal benefits. Let customers know what the products have done for you and your customers. Then let your prospect know that he or she deserves the best.

Have on hand testimonial letters and technical data to back up your claims. Information and data in writing have more credibility. People need to see it to believe it, as the saying goes.

Activity: Price Objections

Work with your upline on a good answer to the price objections you may hear in your business. Memorize and internalize the answers. Role play those with your upline until you can give them without thinking.

Customer Retention

Most network marketers spend too much time trying to get new customers and not enough time keeping those they already have. Once you have 10 to 20 customers, you should invest 80% of your retailing time in building long-term relationships with current customers and 20% on finding new customers.

The first step in building a solid relationship is to mail customers a thank-you note after their first purchase. You can buy thank-you notes at office supply or stationery stores. Print shops usually have several choices of stock thank-you notes. What type of impression will a thank-you note leave? When was the last time you received a handwritten thank-you note from a salesperson? Most people have never received one. If you have, how did it make you feel? That's the way your customer will feel. Along with the thank-you note, include a coupon for a discount on the customers next order. This will start them thinking about a next order.

The second step is good follow up. A few days after your customers have received their products, call to see if they have questions and get their feedback. If they have any concerns or problems, remedy them immediately. Show your customers that you care about them and not just their money.

Next, set up a regular call back. When you call for your customers' regular order, have some additional product suggestions. Monthly specials work well, too. Give customers something for an order of a certain size or a discount on certain products.

Make sure you contact your customers immediately when new products are introduced. Offer an introductory discount for a limited time. New products increase your per order volume and income, so it is important to keep your customers informed.

Be a friend to your customers. Keep track of personal information. Send them birthday and anniversary cards. Talk with your customers about their kids, job, vacations, home, and any other topic in which they seem to be interested.

One distributor sends out cards on crazy occasions like Ground Hog Day, Thanksgiving, and Washington's Birthday. He also sends Father's

Day cards to women and Mother's Day cards to men. During the initial conversation, he always gets both the customer's birthday and that of his or her spouse if they have one. He then sends a reminder letter to the spouse or customer two weeks prior to the other's birthday. Of course he includes some gift suggestions and a date by which they would need to be ordered for them to be delivered on time.

Be innovative with your retailing. Have fun and build some good friendships and some solid customers. Establish all of these retailing habits early in your network marketing career and you will never have any problems with personal volumes.

Chapter 5

Prospecting

Explore the Gold Mine

Every top network marketer knows that prospecting is the key to financial freedom. You need to prospect a large number of people — how many depends on how good your company, products, and presentation are. Industry averages indicate that you will recruit about 10% of the people you prospect. So, to sponsor 50 people, you may need to talk with 500. As your presentations become better, and you use more of the leverage tools available, as discussed in Chapter 6, you will recruit more with fewer personal contacts.

The word prospecting means to explore or search about. In the 1800s, people prospected for gold, and in many ways prospecting in network marketing is very similar. You could compare your initial discovery of network marketing to that of discovering a gold mine.

For example, imagine that you are walking in a vacant field and stumble across a shiny rock. Upon closer examination, you discover what appears to be a piece of gold. A jeweler friend of yours confirms that it is indeed gold, and high quality at that. You contact the owner of the property and offer to buy it. He has been trying to sell the old junk lot for years and is happy to part with it for a nominal price.

You borrow some money and begin excavating the area. For the first week your crew digs every day and finds nothing. You are running out of time and money. You begin to doubt your discovery. Maybe there isn't any gold. Could someone have planted that piece of gold just to sell the property? You start to feel like a fool, a broke fool, when in rushes the foreman and announces that they've hit a vein.

It turns out to be the biggest gold strike in history. You are an instant billionaire. There is more gold than you could ever mine, so you decide to share it with all the people you know. You go to everyone you have ever known and tell them about the gold mine. You invite them to purchase the tools and come mine your gold. Anything they get from their own hard work is theirs to keep.

As a network marketer, you have that same gold mine, and now is the time to share it with everyone you have ever known. Remember though, you have the gold and they don't. You don't have to beg them or try to convince them to come dig gold with you. Some are going to think the work is too hard. Others will complain that the tools are too expensive. Many will say they don't have time. A few won't believe you.

Your mission, should you decide to accept it, is to offer the gold to everyone. Share your dream of time freedom, financial security, wealth, and lifestyle. If they can see and feel the dream, they will join you. If they decide not to join you, you do not have to feel disappointed or inadequate. Network marketing does not require you to be a pushy salesperson, either in retailing or prospecting.

Prospecting is an integral part of your business. The better you become as a prospector, the faster your network will grow and the greater the personal and financial rewards. When prospecting, you will work with two groups of people — your warm market and your cold market. In the following sections, you will learn how to prospect effectively in each type of market.

Your Warm Market

If you had that gold mine, wouldn't you want to share it with your family and friends first, and then share it with all the rest of the people you know? Your friends, family, co-workers, business associates, and others you know are called your warm market. Start your network marketing business by sharing your products and opportunity with the people in your warm market. People new to network marketing tend to have an aversion to prospecting their warm market — they fear that their friends and family will think they are crazy for getting involved in "one of those pyramid schemes" and begin avoiding them. This will not happen to you if you approach your friends and family correctly.

If you opened a retail store, would you be afraid to invite the people you know to your new store? What if you had a great tip on a stock that was going to go up. Would you keep it to yourself? If you just went to an excellent movie, would you tell people about it? That is all network marketing is. Don't think of it as selling to your friends, because you are not. You are offering them the opportunity to change their financial future and use superior products that they can't get anywhere else.

Prospect List

The first step in effective prospecting is to make a list. Social scientists say that we know thousands of people, but we just can't remember them all. Start your list with everyone who immediately comes to mind. Don't leave someone out because you think they are too rich, too busy, or too successful. Also, don't leave people out because they have never been successful, have never worked, or are older or younger than you think a successful network marketing should be. If you leave people off your list, for whatever reason, you are making a very big mistake. You never know who will be interested. In fact, most of the people you think will be interested won't be, and those you don't think will be interested will. Don't prejudge anyone — put them all on your list.

After the people who immediately come to mind, move on to people at work, past jobs, clubs, friends of friends, college and high school classmates, teachers, parents of your children's friends. Expand your list by using the memory jogger list in Table 5.1 on page 88.

Don't stop until you have at least 100 names. Five hundred names is even better, and 1,000 or more is best. Remember, don't prejudge anyone. If you leave someone out who could be one of your most successful downline distributors, it costs you. For example, one network marketer precluded a man who was very successful in franchising because she assumed that, because he was so successful, he wouldn't be inter-

Table 5.1: Prospect Memory Jogger

The following list describes people you can add to your warm market prospect list. Think about whom you know who:

- Shows genuine concern for other people.
- Is active in your church.
- Is really friendly and likable.
- Does personal counseling.
- Is a professional.
- Is very active in the community.
- Does volunteer work.
- Deals with many people every day.
- Is in a management or supervisory position.
- Is looking for more out of life.
- Is ambitious.
- Is considered a leader.
- Has children just starting school.
- Owns their own business.
- Is very stressed at their job.
- Has money problems.
- Is very creative.
- Could use some extra money.
- Is going to college or trade school and could use a part-time income.
- Was recently married and just getting started.
- Knows many people.
- Holds an influential position.
- Has international connections.
- Is an elected official.
- Has children and doesn't work outside the home.
- Is in your health club.
- Plays tennis, golf, or goes bowling with you.
- Lived in the old neighborhood.
- Appraised your home.
- Sold you your home.
- Use to live in your home.
- Rents you your apartment.
- Works on your car.
- Is your doctor, dentist, attorney, CPA.
- Is on your Christmas card list.
- Does your hair, nails.
- Delivers your mail, newspaper, packages.
- Sold you your last car.
- Handles your insurance.
- Sells Avon, Tupperware, Mary Kay, or Fuller Brush.
- Does your dry-cleaning.
- Grooms your pets.
- Was in your wedding.
- Was in your fraternity or sorority.
- Is in the PTA with you.
- Is in Rotary, Kiwanis, Lions, or Eagles.
- Teaches your children swimming.
- Is a teller at the bank.
- Is a checker at the grocery store.
- Babysits your kids.
- Works at the daycare center.
- Is your travel agent.

ested in network marketing. Several months later he called to say he had sold his franchises to do network marketing full time. He went on to become tremendously successful.

Now take a moment to start your prospect list. The following activity will help you get started.

Activity: Prospect List

Stop right now and make your list. The bigger your list, the longer it will take before you have to get into the cold market. Remember not to pre-judge anyone! Put them all on your list and then give a copy to your sponsor. Discuss each person with your sponsor and develop a plan for prospecting each of them.

Methods of Contact

Now that you have your list, you are ready to consider how to contact prospects. Talk with you sponsor or upline leader about their recommended method. Most companies offer video and audio tapes you can mail to prospects along with a personal note. Some of the newer companies offer 24-hour information lines and fax-on-demand services. You can mail a letter to people on your list that describes your company, your products, and how network marketing works. Try to create curiosity, and then request that they call the message line or fax-on-demand line.

While both of these approaches are great and easy, they will probably produce only marginal results. The best method of contact is to call prospects and tell them you have discovered gold and want to share it with them. If your upline person is good at prospecting and interested in helping you, have him or her do three-way calls with you to the first few prospects until you feel more comfortable.

On the phone, you can take one of three approaches:

- The direct approach — "I've discovered a tremendous financial opportunity and want to share it with you."

- The opinion approach — "I think I've discovered a tremendous financial opportunity and would like your input."
- The referral approach — "I've discovered a tremendous financial opportunity, do you know anyone who would like to dramatically increase their income base?"

If you are concerned about appearing pushy with your friends, the third approach is the best. If your friends are curious or interested, they will tell you. Otherwise they will give you referrals or just say they can't think of anyone.

Preparing for the Call

Prior to making the call, work with your sponsor or upline leader to develop a script. It should include the following six steps:

- Pardon the time intrusion — For example, you might say, "Do you have a minute to talk?" "Am I catching you at a bad time?" or "Do you have a few minutes?"
- Compliment — You will always have much better results if you compliment your prospect's business or personal skills. For example, "Tom, I've always respected you as a businessperson. You're a sales manager right?"
- Create curiosity — "Tom, I think I've discovered gold and I'd like to share it with you. Are you interested in dramatically increasing your income?"
- Control the conversation — Most network marketers find that if they answer a prospect's questions, the prospect will just end the conversation by saying no. A better approach is to avoid answering questions, to end each statement with a question of your own, and to get a commitment from the prospect that he or she will listen to a tape or attend a presentation.
- Get a commitment — Try to get your prospect to promise to call an information line, to look at or listen to a tape, to listen in on a teleconference, to meet with you, or to attend a presentation. For example, "Tom, you really need to look at this. It's a two step process. The first is to get you oriented by..."

- Confirm with posture — Many people will say yes, but not mean it. Some prospects may agree to look at your products or to attend a presentation, but you will waste a good deal of time waiting for people who never show up. You will also spend a lot of money on materials and postage in mailing materials to people who ask you to mail something, even though they are really not interested. You've got the gold. You decide, not them. Confirm an appointment with a prospect in a way that assures he or she will really follow through. For example, "Tom, I'll look forward to seeing you at the Hilton on Friday at 7:00 P.M. Do you have that on your calendar? Seating is reserved, so I'm going to reserve a seat in your name. Before I do that, if you can think of any reason why you couldn't make it, please let me know now, so I can give your seat to someone else."

When new network marketers, and sometimes those who have experience, read these six steps, they sometimes find them controlling or pushy. This approach is designed to put you in control, and it is also an approach proven by all the top money earners in network marketing. All have tried other, softer approaches, and found them to be unsuccessful nearly every time. Rather than thinking of this approach as pushy, think of it as caring. If you tell your prospect too much, or do not control the conversation and get an appointment, the prospect will not look at your business. You both lose in that case. You cannot show a prospect a network marketing opportunity over the phone; it must be done in person or with a professionally produced video tape. The telephone approach described above is the proven method in network marketing that leads to an in-person presentation.

This approach works for several reasons. First, an organized approach creates confidence in the prospect. Second, when you control the conversation, you don't give the prospect time to vacillate — if the prospect hesitates or becomes confused, he or she will likely say no. Third, your approach is confident and complete. You will have planned your approach carefully with your upline leader or sponsor to assure that the prospect knows everything he or she needs to know at this point. When you let the prospect control the conversation, you will not deliver the information you need to. Finally, this approach works because it creates curiosity, but does not satisfy it. If you stimulate someone's curiosity and then give them the opportunity to satisfy it — by attending a presentation or watching a video — they will decide to take the next step, to find out more information, nearly every time.

The Call

Now you're ready for the call. For the first few prospecting calls, you will be nervous, but that is natural. Prospecting will get easier with each call. Pick up the receiver, smile, and dial. Maintain a friendly, conversational tone, but put some extra enthusiasm in your voice. Your enthusiasm alone can create curiosity.

Have your script in front of you, follow it exactly, and keep the conversation brief. Most likely they will ask questions or throw out an objection to see how you react or how firmly dedicated to the idea you are. Along with your script, have in front of you a list of the most common questions and objections with the answers. The following list of common questions and objections will help prepare you for what you will face during your prospecting calls. Consider the following responses, or work out different answers yourself or with your sponsor.

- Tell me more — If your prospect asks for more information, you will have more success convincing them of the legitimacy of the business if you invite them to a seminar or meet with them in person to display your products or show them your company literature. For example, you might say, "Mary, I'm so excited that I could go on for hours, there's so much I want to tell and show you, but neither of us have that kind of time on the phone right now. Let's set a time to get together. How about (day) at (time)?" or "Tom, this is big business and you and I both know you can't do big business on the phone. Let's get together. How about (day) at (time)?"

- What company? — Bill, it's XYZ company, have you heard of them?" Wait for the answer and say, "It's a tremendous financial opportunity, I know you're going to be impressed. Let's get together on (day) at (time)."

- Is it MLM? — "Absolutely! Did you know that major publications, like *Success* and *Entrepreneur*, plus many top business analysts and leading edge economists are saying that MLM or network marketing is the best wealth building vehicle available to the average person?

We need to meet and talk about this, it's big! How about (day) at (time)?"

- Is it Amway? — If you are in Amway, say, "Absolutely! Did you know that Amway did over X billion dollars in revenues last year and that we currently operate in X countries. You need to take a look at this. Let's get together. How about (day) at (time)?" If you are not in Amway, say, "No. You need to take a look at this. It's hot! Let's get together. How about (day) at (time)?"

- I'm too busy! —— "That's exactly why I called you. Busy people make things happen in this business, and you are perfect. You need to take a look at this. It's hot! Let's get together. How about (day) at (time)?"

- Is it sales? — A network marketer does not need to like or dislike sales, or to be good or bad at sales. You can diffuse this objection by asking, "Do you like sales?" If their answer is yes, say, "You're going to love this!" If their answer is no, say,"You're going to love this!" Let the prospect decide for himself or herself whether the similarity of network marketing to sales is a pro or a con. Get the prospect to commit to learning more. "You need to take a look at this business. It's hot! Let's get together. How about (day) at (time)?"

- Not interested — "I wouldn't expect you to be. At this point you don't have enough information. In fact I don't even know whether you qualify yet. The first step is to get you oriented to the company. Let's get together. How about (day) at (time)?"

Even when you do your best and handle their questions or objections effectively, many will still say no. It's their loss! Remember you still have the gold mine. They just turned down the opportunity to dig. Keep talking with people, and you will find many who recognize the tremendous opportunity you are presenting.

Product

Any time a prospect says no, immediately move on to talk about your products. Not everyone will be interested in becoming a distributor, but that does not mean they might not be interested in the products you sell. Retail sales create income for you. Also, many top distributors enter network marketing after being a retail customer first. When the products are good, retail customers often sign up to become distributors.

Many network marketers have trouble making the transition from prospecting new distributors to prospecting retail customers. The best way is to ask a question. For example, if you market nutritional products, you might ask, "Are you concerned about your health?" or "Would you like to have more energy?" This makes a nice lead-in to your standard product statements, as described in Chapter 4.

Referrals

After you have either transitioned into products successfully or received another no, ask for referrals. For example, you might say, "Whom do you know who might like to make some extra money or improve their health?" These referrals will be excellent leads, so work hard to get them. Richard Kall, one of the most successful network marketers in history, built his huge network almost totally on referrals because he was uncomfortable talking with strangers. He says to get down on your knees and beg for referrals. If you ask, they will come.

Follow Up

Most people whom you prospect will refuse to look at your products or to consider the network marketing opportunity. In fact, 80% or more of the prospects you talk to will turn you down. Some will decline because they are not open-minded. Some are just at the wrong time in their lives. Some are too stressed to even listen. Others have a misconception about network marketing. Whatever the situation, eventually they will change their minds. You need to follow up in order to catch a prospect at a more opportune moment.

Many people who are very negative about network marketing change their minds when something happens in their lives — layoff, firing, sexual harassment, injury, reduction in pay, increase in sales quota, reduction of sales territory, demotion, illness, relocation, divorce, bankruptcy, or forced early retirement. Even though some people are not willing to take a look now, they may be some day soon. Your job is to stay in touch until the timing is right.

If you start with a good warm list, follow up effectively, and continue to ask for referrals, you may never have to enter your cold market.

Unfortunately, most people run out of people on their warm list in about a week. If your goal is to achieve financial independence, you will need to move to the cold market.

Contacting in the Cold Market

The cold market contains all the people you do not know — all the people outside your widest circle of even casual acquaintances. There are 270 million people in the United States, and nearly all are now accessible to you — by mail, telephone, fax, computer online services, or in person. The key to getting contacts in the cold market is to develop a system that allows you to quickly sift through all those potential prospects to find people who are interested and at the right time in their lives to participate in your network of distributors.

Much of what you have already learned about prospecting in the warm market applies in the cold market. However, the cold market is much harder to work. Your closing percentages will be about 30% in the warm market and 10% in the cold market.

You can find people everywhere to whom you can present your ideas, so you will never lack prospects. What you will lack is contacts. The key is to develop a plan that will, when implemented, generate sufficient leads to produce enough distributors for you to reach your goals. Sit down with your sponsor or upline leader and discuss your goals. Determine how many distributors you need to meet your goals, how many presentations you need to give to recruit a distributor, and how many contacts you need to get a presentation. Then evaluate your time and the number of direct contacts you will make. Subtract that from the total contacts, and you have the number that your plan must generate.

The following sections describe some ways to generate leads in the cold market. Some methods are very similar to methods of retailing, described in Chapter 4, and to methods of prospecting in the warm market, described earlier in this chapter. However, you will need to practice some slightly different techniques in the cold market, as described in the remainder of this chapter.

Telephone

If you can get beyond your own fear, cold calling can be very effective. You can call either residences or businesses. All people are prospects, so talk with whomever answers the phone, unless it is obviously a child. You can also target owners or managers, real estate or insurance salespeople, doctors or nurses. Pick up the phone book and you instantly have the names of thousands of prospects.

When you call, begin your conversation with, "Hi (their name), this is (your name), do you have a moment to talk?" If they say no, ask for a time to call back. If they ask what it is regarding, go right into the script. They may ask how you got their name. Be truthful — say you got it from the directory, off a business card, from a referral, or whatever your source is.

If the person does have time to talk, begin with, "I am a recruiter for a young growth company that is expanding into the area. We are looking for a couple of key leaders. Are you open to a financial opportunity that could make you a lot of money and not affect your current situation?" If the prospect is interested, get a commitment to listen or watch a tape, call your 24-hour information line or the fax-on-demand line, meet with you, attend a business orientation, listen to a national teleconference, or watch a satellite conference.

If you have a fax machine and the prospect indicates interest, ask if they have a fax machine nearby. If they do, tell them you will fax some preliminary information and call back in about an hour. Fax them an information sheet on your opportunity — the information fax is described in more detail in Chapter 6 on presentations. An effective cold call, followed by an information fax, can produce instant results.

Walking and Talking

If you are the type of person who loves to meet new people, the walking and talking method of prospecting is the perfect method for you. In your daily life, try to become more aware of the people with whom you come in contact. You can approach these people directly or indirectly. The most direct approach to cold market prospecting is to introduce yourself and ask a question, such as:

Do you consider yourself an open-minded person?;

Are you open to an idea that could dramatically increase your income base?;

Are you interested in making some very serious money?;

Are you making as much money as you would like?; or

Do you have as much time freedom as you would like?

All of these questions have been used by successful distributors. They are designed to open a conversation and pre-qualify people by assessing their attitude about a new idea or financial opportunity. If you don't like any of these, make up your own qualifying question. If a prospect answers your question with a yes, set up a time to meet, invite them to a group presentation, give them a tape, or get an address so you can mail some information.

A second method is less direct. You make the same approach, but instead of immediately presenting your idea, you just start a conversation. "How long have you worked here?" "Do you come here often?" "How old are your kids?" "What do you do for a living?" Carry on a brief, rapport-building conversation, and then comment that you have a financial opportunity that might interest them. Ask for their business card or name, address, and phone number so that you can send them some information. Mail them a letter, prospectus, mailer, or tape. Follow up with a phone call within 72 hours.

Malls are great places to walk and talk. You can go into the stores and talk with salespeople or sit on the benches and talk with people near you. If you have kids, take them with you. Many malls have areas where the children can play. While they play, you can start a conversation with the other parents. If the weather is nice, playgrounds and parks can be great too. Parents are always sitting around waiting for their kids to get tired or bored. A great number of full-time moms have used these methods for building successful networks.

Another method of prospecting the cold market is to go to your local coffee shop and sit at the counter. Early in the morning you will catch the salespeople and managers. Later in the day, you will catch the unemployed. Sit next to someone who looks promising and introduce yourself. Then ask what they do for a living. They will then return the question, so you will need to have a standard answer that will create curiosity. "I'm involved in health and wealth, which would you like to hear about first?" Again, this is a prospecting method for those who love to meet new people, so if you are not afraid to talk to people you don't know, this can be a very effective method of prospecting.

Walking and talking is a prospecting method that has been used by thousands of top distributors. It is certainly only one of many successful prospecting methods, but it is one that can be very effective. Try going out to look for new friends instead of new distributors. You are searching for people who have the same interests that you do — to become successful and achieve financial and time freedom.

Advertising

Advertising for prospects is a method you should use after you have been in network marketing for at least a year. When you place a classified ad, you will get calls from people looking for jobs. They will ask very pointed questions, such as the name of the company, how much money they can make, and if it is one of those pyramid deals. If you are not a seasoned veteran who has learned how to handle these questions, you will lose most of these leads. On the other hand, if you know what to say, advertising can be a tremendous lead generator.

Talk with your sponsor or upline leader about whether or not you should use advertising to get leads. If you are ready to use advertising, write a short classified ad, such as:

MAKE EXTRA $$$
PT/FT. Training provided.
Management potential.
Call 555-5555
24-hour recorded message

Have them call into a dedicated voice mail box and listen to a one- or two-minute information message. The message should be exciting, create interest, and do some pre-qualification. However, don't try to sell the caller on network marketing on your message. Ask callers to leave their name and number so you can give them additional information.

Prospecting Cards

Prospecting cards are business cards that have a prospecting message on them. For example, your card might read like this:

MAKE SERIOUS MONEY
in your spare time.
For more information call
our 24-hour recorded message
555-5555
If you have the guts to call
it could make you rich!

Black ink on a white card is the most economical. Have at least 1,000 printed because you will need to distribute 100 to get one good lead. You may get many calls, but only about 1% will be interested enough to leave a name and number on your voice mail.

The most effective way to distribute prospecting cards is to go to the business district at about 7:30 A.M. and hand out cards to people heading into work. Extend your arm with a card in your hand and say, "I am an executive recruiter looking for talent for a young growth company. You look like the type of person we need. If you would like to know more, call the number on the card."

You can also put them on the windows of parked cars. Put them on the driver side window, rather than the windshield. This way they will see it prior to getting in the car. Many people will call from their cellular phone.

You might also leave prospecting cards in phone booths, restrooms, and community bulletin boards. Prospecting cards are also great to include in your bill payment envelopes, junk mail envelopes, or even in a plain white envelope to mail to people. They will wonder who sent it to them and call out of curiosity.

Many successful network marketers have very good results handing prospecting cards out at the airport. Pick a city where you would like to start a group. Look on the departure and arrival boards for flights to and from that city. Go and sit in the waiting area and look for people who seem to have a great attitude. Walk up to them and say, "Excuse me, but I couldn't help noticing that you have great attitude. I'm a recruiter for a young growth company. We are looking for people with great attitudes who would like to make some very serious money. Here's my card. If you would like to know more, call the number on the card. Thanks for taking the time to talk with me. Have a great day." You might also ask for their business card or name and number. You could build a national and international organization from your local airport.

As you are preparing to leave the airport, make sure you leave a small stack of prospecting cards at every pay telephone, in the business service areas, on the candy and pop machines, on the newspaper machines, and in the restrooms by the sink. You can recruit several people who just picked up a card and called.

Audio Business Card

An audio business card is a more expensive version of the prospecting card. Find an opportunity cassette that has been produced by one of the top money earners in your company. Have your local print shop print cassette labels with a title like, "Your Key to Financial Freedom," plus your name and phone number. Hand these tapes out just like you would the prospecting cards. Introduce yourself the same way you would handing out a prospecting card or making a cold call to get the best results. If you are willing to invest the money, and you have an excellent audio tape, the audio business card can be a very effective prospecting tool.

Poster

Another method to attract cold market prospects is to make up an 8½" x 11" poster with a headline like, "You're Either Interested In Getting Rich or Your Not." Then add some more curiosity-building phrases, like, "If you've been looking for that perfect wealth-building vehicle, call the number below for a very exciting message." Include your voice mail number, and leave room at the bottom for small strips, with "Get Rich" and the voice mail number on each that prospects can rip off and take with them. Print your poster on a bright paper — ask the printer for Astrobright — and tape or tack them in phone booths, telephone poles, and community bulletin boards.

Flyers

Many network marketers prefer to use ½ sheet flyers, 5½" x 8½", printed on bright paper. You can use the same kind of message as on the poster, but set them up two on a page, print 500 and cut them, so you end up with 1,000. Take them to the business district and give them to people or put them on cars. Park and ride lots are also good locations. You can cover a larger number of cars in a shorter period of time.

Direct Mail

Two types of direct mail work well in network marketing. The first is called cooperative, which is similar to cooperative coupons discussed in Chapter 4 on retailing. Another form of cooperative direct mail is the "card deck." These cards are about the size of a 3 x 5 card. Generally, 30 to 50 cards are mailed together to targeted lists. You pay for one card, so it is pretty economical.

The second type is targeted direct mail in which you either build or secure a list of prospects, and then send a personalized mailer to them. Targeted direct mail is much more expensive, but you get a higher response rate for your investment. With a quality mail piece and a good offer, you could get as high as a 10% response.

Another direct mail approach is the secret letter. Type a generic letter describing the benefits of your products or opportunity. Mail these to people whose names you retrieve from the phone book, business directories, association membership lists, or other types of directories. Send them in a plain white envelope. Make sure you give recipients several options, either to call the 24-hour information line, listen in on a national teleconference, call the fax-on-demand line, or request a free tape. Send out ten of these each day and you will be amazed at how many prospects you have.

Voice Mail and Answering Machine Calls

Many of the new network marketing leaders find this method to be the most productive at the lowest cost. Write a short script in which you speak for about one minute describing the benefits of your opportunity. Call residences between 10 A.M. and 2 P.M. looking for voice mail or answering machines. If a person answers, you can prospect them or, if you feel uncomfortable talking with people, just say you have the wrong number.

For example, a sample script that has worked well for many network marketers is the following:

> Hello, my name is (your name), and I'm involved with an international company that is working on a multi-million dollar marketing deal here in the area. This may appear to be a little off the wall since it doesn't have anything to do with your business; however, I'm working closely with people in your industry, and the bottom line is the same anyway — financial return.
>
> I am looking for a couple of key partners for this venture. No, I'm not looking for investors, but rather people who can spend five to ten hours per week to help build and manage a marketing team. If this is done properly, we will all achieve total financial freedom within the next three to five years.
>
> If you are at the right time in your life for a new challenge — one that will not jeopardize your current situation — and if this sounds interesting, call me at 555-5555 so that we can set up an informational interview. Again, my name is (your name), and the number is 555-5555. I highly recommend that you check this out. This is not a joke and you have absolutely nothing to lose by calling.
>
> Thank you for listening to this message. I look forward to your call.

You can also call businesses late at night and on weekends. Sunday is a great day to spend an hour or two calling. Use the same type of message as you use for the residential calls.

Distributors who consistently make these calls every day get a 10% to 20% response. Would you like to have 72 leads each month? Make 30 voice mail calls each day, six days per week. At a 10% response, you will have 72 leads.

Door Hangers

You can use door hangers for either retailing or recruiting. For retailing, you might put a catalog or brochure and a sample in a plastic bag to hang on a resident's door knob. For recruiting, you will need to work with a print shop to make up card stock door hangers. Use a message similar to the one you might use on a poster or flyer, described earlier. Print up at least 1,000 door hangers and walk from house to house. You will get about a 1% response, so the larger the number you distribute, the better.

Executive Letter

Executive letters are another excellent producer of leads, but you really need to have a computer to make this one work. First, you'll need a list of businesspeople — owners, managers, upper level executives, and salespeople. Enter those names into a database and set up a standardized prospecting letter. In the letter, your first paragraph should grab the reader's attention and create interest. The second paragraph should list a few of the benefits of your program. The third paragraph should give them options for contacting you or obtaining more information. A sample of an executive letter is shown on page 104.

If you use this method, commit to mailing at least ten letters per day. A good word processing program should have a mail merge feature, allowing you to type the list of people and the letter separately, and the computer will merge the two automatically. With this feature, you can produce many letters quickly, and each will look as though it was typed specifically for the person. A good letter will generate a 10% to 20% response, so consistent daily mailings will produce a tremendous number of new prospects.

Public Speaking

If you enjoy public speaking, you might consider developing a talk that would establish you as an expert in your field. Offer to speak at chamber of commerce functions, Rotary, Kiwanis, trade associations, business fairs and conferences, and corporate meetings. Contact your local chamber of commerce office for a list of business organizations and associations. If a phone number is listed, call for the person in charge of booking speakers. If only an address is given, type up an outline of your talk and your credentials and mail it to the address listed. If you would like to contact businesses for corporate meetings,

Sample Executive Letter

March 19, 1995

Susan Smith
New Your Life Insurance Company
1200 First Plaza
Anytown, USA 55555

Dear Susan:

I have recently become a business partner in a multi-million dollar marketing venture that has absolutely incredible financial potential for those involved. We believe that the people who are involved in this carefully researched, ground floor business could literally make a fortune over the next three to five years! We are not looking for financial partners or investors, but rather people who will work with us on the venture (this would work well in conjunction with your present operation). We need people, like you, who are too busy to take on anything else, highly motivated, open-minded, goal-oriented, and ethical. We need people who can recognize a good opportunity when they see one.

I have recommended you as a potential partner because of my respect for you as a businessperson, which is the reason for this formal method of contact. If you are ready to create a permanent income stream, a potential of $50,000 to $100,000 per month, and would like the time freedom to enjoy it, then give me a call. We have prepared a video prospectus that will outline this venture. Once you have reviewed the tape, we can talk, and I will answer any questions you may have.

I do not want you to feel pressured. Therefore, unless you contact me regarding this matter, I will not call to follow up. I do, however, encourage you to at least take the time to look at the tape and research this business with an open mind — I know you will be as pleased as I have been. We expect to take on between five and ten new partners, so if you are interested, please respond promptly.

Thank you for your time, and I hope to hear from you soon.

Sincerely,

Rod Nichols

contact the human resources department and ask to speak with the person who books speakers for their meetings.

Another effective prospecting method is to set up public seminars and charge a small fee to cover the advertising costs and meeting room. Book a room at a local library, meeting hall, or hotel. To market the seminar, you can mail brochures or flyers, advertise in the newspaper, post flyers, call people, or a combination of these methods. Develop a package of handouts that you will give to each attendee. Make sure the fee you charge will cover the cost of marketing the event, renting the room, and printing the handouts.

You can speak on something that relates to your product or industry, or about new trends in marketing, such as network marketing versus linear marketing.

Make sure that you get cards from everyone attending. Giving away a door prize is a great way to assure that you get business cards from attendees. You can also ask people to complete an information sheet if they would like to be on your mailing list or exchange a cassette for their business card.

Fishbowl

Many businesses collect business cards as a method of entering people in a contest. If you are at a restaurant and see a fishbowl full of business cards, ask the manager what they do with the cards when the contest is over. If they throw them away, tell him or her that you collect business cards and would appreciate it if you could pick them up. An alternative method is actually to place a fishbowl in a restaurant. Give away a meal each week or month. To set up a bowl, buy a fishbowl at a pet store. Put a sign on the bowl that says to put a business card in the bowl to win a free meal at the restaurant. Start the bowl with a few cards with black dots on the back. People don't like to put their card in an empty bowl. The black dots will help you separate the real cards from those you planted.

Each week or month, pick the winners and call them. This is a good opportunity to prospect them. Then take the rest of the cards and call, using your cold calling script. If you have not prospected the winner, call a week or so after they receive their free meal to see how the meal was. During the call, find out more about them and prospect if they are a good candidate.

Contests

Contests are always a great way to get names. People love to enter contests. Chapter 4 on retailing discussed how you might use a lead box that promotes a contest to get people to put their names and phone numbers in the box. You can use the same concept for recruiting. Use the same box and change the message.

If you want to do something bigger, put together a group of distributors who all contribute funds. Using direct mail, offer a contest to win a trip to Hawaii or Mexico. To cut costs, you could do this in conjunction with a radio station and high traffic retailer. Contact the marketing department of the radio station or retailer, explain your contest, the number of people who will receive your mailing, and solicit their sponsorship — a financial donation, air time on the radio station, or a product or service to be given as a prize. After the contest is over, collect the names and give them to each participating distributor so that they can call and prospect the person. Because there are regulations regarding contests, contact your local authorities for the local laws before you get started.

Survey

A survey can be a less confrontive and highly effective recruiting tool. Pick a place that gets a good deal of foot traffic — a shopping mall, shopping center, airport, or grocery store. Make up a survey with no more than ten questions. See example on page 107. You can ask questions about employment, lifestyle, economy, retirement, financial security, or something related to your product. Type the survey and make at least 50 copies.

Take your survey and a clipboard and head for the location you have chosen. Pick out people who seem to be in a positive frame of mind. Step forward and say, "Hi, my name is (your name). We're conducting a survey on employment. Do you have time to answer seven quick questions?" If they don't, thank them and move on to the next person, until you find someone who will participate.

After you have asked the questions, determine whether they are a good prospect. If so, ask if they would be interested in looking at a way that they could double or triple their income and enjoy more time freedom? If they say yes, give them your business card and ask for theirs. At the very least, try to get their name and number. You may also want to give them an audio or video tape. Another possibility is to give them a prospecting card, discussed on page 99, and request that they call for more information.

Example Survey: Employment

1. What is your current occupation?

2. How long have you worked in your current occupation?

3. On a scale of 1 to 10, how would you rate satisfaction with your occupation?

4. In your current occupation, can you achieve financial security within the next 10 years?

5. If you could, what would you change about your occupation?

6. Have you ever considered starting your own business?

   (If yes) Did you start a business? What happened? What kept you from starting it?

   (If no) Why haven't you ever considered starting a business?

7. If you discovered a business that could be started for under $100, where you would be trained by a successful business owner, the risk was very minimal, and you would have the potential to develop total time and financial freedom within five years, would you consider it?

   (If yes, offer them an opportunity to look at your business.)

   (If no, tell them thank you for participating in the survey and ask for the names of 2 or 3 people they know who would be willing to participate in the survey.)

Career Centers

Most high schools and colleges have career centers where they list jobs for students. You can advertise for students who would like to earn extra income in their own part-time business. You can advertise that you provide full training and that the job has management potential.

Since students are in need of income and a flexible work schedule, network marketing is perfect for them. Also, because many students are having a difficult time these days finding good jobs after high school and college, they tend to be open-minded to a viable alternative.

If you can recruit one student leader, he or she can assist you in adding other bright, motivated students to your network. You may want to try to identify leaders in student politics, athletics, drama, or other popular student activities. Make contact with them, introduce them to the concept of network marketing, and explain how much they can learn about operating a business under your mentorship.

A Resident Assistant (R.A.) in a college dorm can be a good contact, particularly if he or she allows you to make a presentation in the dorm. R.A.s are responsible for overseeing dorm activities. They are older students who get paid only a small amount for their job in the dorms. They can be very good prospects, or, at the very least, can probably give you some good referrals.

Occasionally, schools have career fairs in which you can participate. These fairs give you an opportunity to meet large numbers of students who are pre-qualified because they are looking for a job.

You may also find good prospects in the people who staff career centers. These people have been trained to help students find jobs. Generally they have outstanding people skills, but are poorly paid. You can help them help more people and augment their income at the same time.

Employment Agencies and Personnel Managers

Employment agencies get thousands of calls from job seekers. They have to turn many callers away for one reason or another. These are potential prospects for you. Call and talk with the owner of the agency. Tell them that you are a consultant who has devised a way for employment agencies to increase revenues without changing the operation or time commitment. Ask the owner if he or she would be interested in hearing about it. Explain that it will take 30–45 minutes and can't be done over the phone. Set up an appointment to meet.

When you arrive, spend the first few minutes of the meeting finding out about the agency — how long have they been in business, how many clients they work with each month, what the agents likes and dislikes about the business. Next, lay out your program and explain the concept of network marketing. Show the owner how he or she could refer people to you and that you would recruit them under the agency.

If they accept and become distributors, help recruit three to five people, and then show the owners how they could increase the numbers by also recruiting. Show them how that could impact their income. Since they have already seen some success and have a small network, you are more likely to get full cooperation.

You can do the same thing with personnel managers, sales managers, and anyone else who is in charge of hiring people. They always have to turn people away. This gives them an avenue for referral.

Buttons, T-Shirts, Hats

Many people who enter network marketing are too shy to approach people directly. A button is a great way for shy people to recruit. Make up a button that says, "I'm Getting Rich! Ask Me How." or "Ask Me About BIG $$$." Wear the button every day. At first it will feel like you are wearing a billboard, but after a while you won't even know it's there.

When people ask, and they will, you need to have a quick line that will stimulate interest. Then ask a commitment-type question. For example, if you wear a button that says, "I'm Getting Rich! Ask Me How," you could respond by saying, "I've found the most amazing financial vehicle. I'm literally getting richer while we're standing here. Does that sound interesting to you?" If they answer yes, get their name and number. If they seem like a good prospect, you might even give them an audio or video tape.

T-shirts and hats work the same way. Mark Yarnell, one of the top network marketers in the country, has a shirt that says, "Ask me about my 1,000 lb. Dog." Do you think that would get some attention? His market research showed that someone who wore the shirt at a mall would get asked about it an average of once every fifteen minutes. If you just walked around for six hours a day, you would end up with 24 leads per day!

Be creative. Think about what would attract you. Ask other people what they would respond to on a button, t-shirt, or hat. Consistency is the key — wear your message every day.

Tradeshow

For prospecting, you probably do not want to get a booth at a tradeshow unless it is a business tradeshow or career fair. The better way to work tradeshows is to go in as a prospect. Talk with the vendors about their products or services. Get their business card. Make a few notes about the person and move on.

At a big tradeshow, like a home show, boat show, auto show, or RV show, you can gather 200 to 300 cards in a day. Wait for about two weeks to contact these people. Right after the show they will be following up on their own leads. By the time you contact them, they will be discouraged by the lack of results from the leads and will be very open to a way they could add to their income base. Make sure you use the information you wrote on the card when you call. Say, "hi (their name), this is (your name). We met at the (name of the tradeshow) about two weeks ago. Do you have time to talk?" They will almost always say yes, because they think you are a prospective buyer. "You probably don't remember me, but I was very impressed with you because... (whatever you wrote on the card). I am a recruiter for a young growth company that is expanding into this area. We are in need of a couple of key leaders and I think you've got what it takes to be one of those. Would you consider an alternative to your current employment?" They will probably ask what the alternative is. You must have memorized a quick statement, such as "I'm working with a company called XYZ. They are growing very rapidly and people are making some very serious money." Or you could work out an answer with your sponsor. Then close with the promise to get them more information.

Lead Exchange

Most cities and towns have lead exchange clubs. Look in the business section of your newspaper or call the chamber of commerce for locations. Lead exchange clubs are groups of businesspeople who meet weekly to exchange leads. Attend all of the clubs in your area and look for one with some aggressive members. It will take a while to establish yourself in one of these clubs, but once you do, you can generate a large number of leads each week. Plus, you can prospect the ever changing membership of the lead exchange clubs.

If you cannot find any lead exchange groups in your area, then start one. Make a list of people or positions within a company who would come into contact with large numbers of people each week. Call the people on your list and offer them membership in your exclusive — only one person from each industry — lead club. When you call businesses, ask for a particular position and ask for the top person. Explain the benefits of your club and offer a membership. Set up a weekly location. If you have members who are not coming to meetings or producing leads, replace them with other people in that industry who might be more productive members of your lead exchange club.

Computer Online Services

If you have a computer with a modem, you can market your business online through America Online, Prodigy, Compuserve, and the many other online services available. These services charge only a small monthly fee and, on some of the services, a fee to advertise. However, this is very inexpensive advertising, and you can reach a large number of people worldwide via online advertising. Best of all, it produces excellent results.

Online advertising is a particularly good medium if your company is expanding internationally. For example, one distributor whose company was expanding into Mexico, put a small ad on America Online and received 30 qualified responses.

Referral Sources

Referrals always close more quickly than cold contacts, so get as many as you can. An excellent way to build a large referral base is to set up a network of referral sources. Referral sources are people who are in contact with many different people every week. Sales clerks, insurance or real estate agents, and bankers are all excellent referral sources. Set up a time to give your presentation to any of these types of customers or prospects. Then ask if they can refer you to people they know or work with that you could contact.

For example, one network marketer found that her insurance agent was not interested in being a distributor for her company, but that he was able to refer an average of two to three high quality candidates every month. Of course, the network marketer calls to check in with the insurance agent about every other week. He now expects her calls and is ready with names.

Cultivate these sources. Take them to lunch, send them a thank you note every time you get a referral, and tell them how much you appreciate working with them. Continue to present information to them just to keep them informed. You never know what life event might turn a referral source into a prospect.

Activity: Prospecting

Select three - five of the prospecting methods and write a brief statement describing how you will prospect for distributors.

Language, Personality, and Personal Style

Now that you have a multitude of ways to create leads, you are ready to start talking with people. Your ultimate success in recruiting depends on your ability to make yourself understood in the clearest, least-threatening way possible. You need to know what approach your prospects will respond best to, and how to speak their language. These are the tools of any sales or recruiting trade. The remainder of this chapter discusses how to recognize certain personality types, and how to best approach prospects who exhibit certain characteristics to assure the best results.

Avoid Industry Jargon

When you begin to discuss the details of network marketing, the parts of it you love best, you may lapse into speaking the jargon of the trade, talking about downlines, uplines, sidelines, and hairlines. If you start throwing around PVs, BVs, and GSVs, you will lose the prospect's attention, and most likely their interest as well. Get rid of the lingo and speak good old English to your prospects.

A number of words are commonly used in network marketing that really turn people off. Table 5.2 illustrates what they are and which alternatives produce better results.

Table 5.2: Certain Words Get Results

Don't Use	Use
Meeting	Briefing, orientation, consultation, interview
Involved	Started
Business opportunity	Financial opportunity
Upline	Mentor, partner, associate
Downline	Partner, associate
Bonuses	Residual or royalty income
MLM or Network Marketing	Mini-franchising concept
Selling	Sharing

Personalities

Effective sponsoring requires that you understand people and work with them in the way that is best for them. As you meet with people, you will discover different personalities. In fact, various studies have isolated four distinct personalities, so if you are dealing with all people in the same way, you are only handling a quarter of the people correctly. No person is ever totally one personality. We are all mixtures, but you will discover that people operate primarily in one of the four types. The four personality types you will most likely encounter and the associated characteristics are described below.

- Analytical — Analytical types like to deal with facts and details. They are very money- and numbers-oriented; they want to know the bottom-line before they will seriously consider any venture, particularly a financial one. They work best independently, are neat and organized, are sticklers for timeliness, and don't much like to take risks.

- Driver — Driver types like to get right to the point of any discussion. They are always busy and always in a hurry. They like immediate results and are willing to take risks to get them. Drivers like to have many choices in front of them — they don't want to be boxed into a corner. They like to be in control, to have power, to be in the driver's seat, as you might guess from the name. Drivers work best independently, and they like to focus on the positive in a situation.

- Amiable — Amiable types like to build relationships. They are friendly and likable, and they cultivate the support of others. They make careful decisions, and they are not risk takers. They are less time-oriented than drivers or analyticals, and they often appear to be wishy-washy in their commitments or in their decision making.

- Expressive — Expressive types are often characterized as dreamers. They like to rely on hunches and gut feelings when they make decisions. They are willing to take risks, but they also like to plan. They tend to focus on the general rather than the specific, they are not particularly time-oriented, and they need to be with people.

As you deal with people in your retailing and prospecting activities, you need to recognize the personality style you operate in and the personality style the people around you operate in. Below are some ways to recognize each personality.

- Analytical and Amiable — People who fall somewhere between these two personality types tend to ask a lot of questions, speak softly, move slowly, and make very little eye contact or hand gestures when they speak. They often lean back in their chair. They can generally be characterized as patient, cooperative, and calm.

- Driver and Expressive — People who exhibit characteristics of both of these personality types generally tell you things rather than ask questions, speak loudly, have fast movements, make direct eye contact, and lean toward you in conversation. They tend to have animated hand gestures while they are talking. In general, they are impatient, competitive, excitable, enthusiastic, and outwardly positive.

- Analyticals and Drivers — People who fall into either of these personality types are less responsive, exhibit a serious attitude, very few facial expressions, and rigid, calculated movements. They have a formal mannerisms, will probably not touch you during conversation, prefer direct conversation, and rarely indulge in chit chat. They also have a heavy time-orientation.

- Amiables and Expressives — These personality types tend to be more responsive than analyticals or drivers, so you will notice more personal questions, a warm, friendly approach, animated expressions, and changes in tone and pitch. They are more likely to touch you in conversation, to be chatty, to make hand gestures, and to have fluid movements.

Begin studying the people in your life to determine their personality type. Take notes and compare them to the characteristics listed in this section. The more you study personalities and the better you understand how to recognize them, the better you will do in business and in life.

Next, you need to know how best to handle each personality type. If you can recognize, if only generally, which personality type your prospect fits in, you will be able to perform in a way that is most appropriate for and most pleasing to that prospect. If your prospect seems to be a driver, don't engage in idle chit chat. Your prospect will get frustrated, tend not to take you seriously, and lose interest quickly. On the other hand, if your prospect seems to fit into the amiable category, try to establish a friendly rapport early on, to take your time during the presentation or conversation, and to be reassuring. Below you will find some helpful tips for how to handle all four personality types.

- Analyticals want facts — If you are working with an analytical type, let them feel they are right, give them facts first, and stress the rational and logical facts. Be sure to observe time constraints and to give quick, precise answers. Compliment them regularly.

- Drivers want to be in control — Drivers tend to be serious and formal, so dress professionally. Get right to the point and don't waste time. Stress results. Because drivers like to be in control, they may lose interest quickly if you lecture. Ask questions that force attention, change voice inflection to maintain interest, and put everything in writing. Let them feel they are in control, and give them choices

- Amiables want to feel sure — Be friendly and build rapport quickly. Talk emotionally. Take your time and don't pressure them. Allow them to include others in decisions and reassure them regularly. Give them one positive choice; if you present too many options they will have difficulty making a decision or be unsure about the decision they made. Help them justify their decision so that they feel good about it.

- Expressives like to dream and plan — Focus on the "big picture." Talk emotionally. Recognize them as being important. Put details in writing and explain carefully. Reassure them regularly.

Recognizing the different personality types and being capable of working with them at their level will make working with people much more fun and produce much better results.

Activity: Types and Characteristics

Write each personality type and its characteristics on a 3" x 5" card. Read them every day until you have them memorized. Analyze the characteristics and determine which personality you operate in while conducting business. Which personality are you? Which personality are the people you know best?

Pick out five people in your life, identify their personality types, and give a brief explanation for why you chose that type. Now, imagine that each of these five people are prospects and give a description, considering your personality type, of how you would approach and work with each person.

Attitudes, Goals, and Motivations

Neurolinguistic programming is the study of the way in which the brain communicates with the nervous system. Over time, everyone builds brain programs that cause us to have certain attitudes or react in a particular way to certain stimuli. Understanding this brain programming can help you in your sales presentations.

Most people are either *externally* or *internally oriented.* If your prospect is very concerned with how other people will feel or see a situation — with peer pressure or peer recognition — then he or she is externally motivated. On the other hand, if the prospect's needs are more personally oriented — toward personal growth or achievement — then he or she is internally motivated. Understanding prospects' motivations will help you determine how to share your product or describe the opportunity to become a distributor. For example, if you were sharing skin care products with a person who is externally motivated, you might stress that other important people are purchasing these products because they think it makes them look younger. The person who had an internal motivation would want to know how the product would help him or her to become better at something or to achieve a personal goal. Again, using the skin care example, you might talk with the person about how your products protect their skin against damage and aging.

Two other types of orientation are *toward the self* and *toward others.* Most people are either programmed with an orientation around themselves or toward other people. If your prospect wants to know what they will gain from the product or from becoming a distributor, then he or she is self-oriented. If the person wants to know how the product will help his or her team or family, they are probably others-oriented. Again, by understanding this orientation, you can make your presentation fit your prospects' attitudes and motivations. Stress the benefits to that individual, if he or she is self- oriented, and the benefits to other people if they are others-oriented.

You might also consider your prospects' motivational movement. People are either *moving toward* or *moving away* from something. The prospect who is moving toward is looking for things that will help them gain. Those who are moving away are trying to find ways to avoid loss. Your presentation terminology will be very important in this area. Stress gain with people who are moving toward and avoidance of loss with those who are moving away.

Sometimes people are programmed to try to find the *likeness* or *the difference* in things. People who try to find the likeness or sameness are called matchers, and those who are always finding the differences are called mismatchers. In a sales presentation, the matcher will try to find other things that they are more familiar with that match your product or opportunity. They will constantly bring up similarities either within your presentation or with other situations. If you show them the similarities, then you build a strong rapport, and they will likely buy from you. The mismatcher will try to find all the things that are inconsistent or wrong. It is your job to head these off by carefully discussing all the details of your product or opportunity and pointing out some of the differences, for example between comparable products or between your product and that of the competitors.

Lastly, many people are motivated by their frame of reference — whether they focus on *what is possible*, or only on *what is necessary*. People who always look for the positive solutions and who are willing to take a calculated gamble in order to gain are possibility thinkers. People who only do what they have to do are necessity thinkers. Stress the potential big gains with possibility thinkers, and only the absolutely necessary with necessity thinkers.

If you want to cater your sales presentation to people according to their particular attitudes, motivations, or personal style, try to develop questions that reveal these aspects of people's personalities. Build these questions into your first contact with the prospect.

Activity: Attitudes, Goals and Motivations

Select two people in your life that you know well. Think up some questions you could ask them to determine their brain program. Call or visit them and ask the questions.

First Contact

Network marketing can sound great and wonderful until you have to pick up the phone and call some prospects. For those first few calls, your telephone receiver will weigh 500 pounds. It will seem impossible to pick up. Your heart will be pounding out of your chest. Your mouth will go dry and your palms will turn clammy.

The cause of these changes is the way in which you are thinking about the phone call you are about to make. Why are you so nervous? You don't want to mess up the call and sound stupid. You are afraid the prospect might think badly of you or ask you questions you can't answer.

These are valid concerns, but you really need to consider what the worst thing is that could happen on that call. If it is someone from your warm market, they will probably tell you they're not interested. If the person is from the cold market, they might be rude to you and hang up. Neither are very pleasant, but do you think you could live through both experiences? Of course you could, so stop all the worrying.

Treat each phone call as a learning experience. Your job is to make the call and learn something. You can't learn anything substantial unless you make some mistakes. In fact, mistakes are a part of the personal growth in this business. Those people who make the most mistakes and learn from them make the most money. That's the only real difference between you and the top achievers in your company. So, make the calls and be happy when you make mistakes. You're just getting closer to financial security.

An excellent way to combat fear is to turn it into excitement. Hopefully, you experience excitement when you make a new friend. Instead of going out every day to find new prospects for your business, go looking for new friends. Then offer your gold mine to your new friends.

Although you may not feel like it at first, you have the power. You don't need to beg people into this business. Don't try to convince them. Don't call in favors or tell them you will do the business for them if they just sign up. You don't want them unless they are ready to make a solid commitment to build a business.

Think of yourself as a manager for Microsoft. Would you beg people to come to work for your company? Of course not! The applicants would have to convince you that they were worthy of working for Microsoft.

Your business is no different. In fact, you offer a much better opportunity. The people you are prospecting must convince you that they are worthy of being chosen a member of your team. They can't reject you, only you can reject them.

The primary reason people do not succeed in network marketing is lack of consistent prospecting. As a serious network marketer, you need to think prospecting all the time. Every time you meet someone, think prospect. Every time you talk with someone on the phone, think prospect.

Some network marketers use a prospecting game called the magic beans. Put ten beans in your left pocket. Every time you prospect someone, move a bean over to your right pocket. When all the beans are moved, you are done prospecting for the day. This is a fun system and it works!

A similar game requires you to take 30 business cards with you each day. Give the cards to anyone within three feet of you, the three-foot rule. When you give out all your cards, you can go home.

One network marketer was using this technique one day and had only given out 15 of her cards by 3:00 on Friday afternoon. She entered an office and asked to speak with the owner. He turned out to be a very large, gruff looking man who towered over her. She handed him her business card and started talking. He took one look at it and tore it into little pieces, which he then deposited on the floor at her feet. She immediately pulled out another card and handed it to him with a big smile. This really made him mad, so he tore this card into even smaller pieces and dropped them on the floor with the others. Once again, she immediately handed him another card and smiled. This went on until she had given him the fifth card. At this point he looked baffled and asked why she kept giving him cards when he just tore them up. She explained that her goal each day was to give 30 business cards to new prospects and that if he kept this up, she could go home early. He laughed and invited her into his office. He became her largest customer and best referral source.

Go out and get some beans or use your business cards, then get out there and prospect every day. Set a daily goal and don't quit until you meet your goal. Everyone you meet is a prospect. Don't prejudge anyone. You never know who will be your next, or first, superstar. Sometimes it is the least likely person. Prospects are all around you. Just look for people who want more out of life. Then help them get it!

International Prospecting

If your network marketing company is not currently involved in the international market, it will be. There are tremendous opportunities internationally. Canada, Hong Kong, Taiwan, Mexico, and Australia are excellent countries for network marketing. Unfortunately, if you are like most distributors, you don't know anyone in any of those countries. If you do that's great, talk with them right away. Even if your company isn't in that country, you can let them know what you are doing and prepare them for when your company does enter their country.

On the other hand, if you don't have any international contacts, you can still capitalize on international growth. Here are some ideas that have resulted in millions of dollars in residuals for international markets.

Think Global, Sponsor Local

The best way to tap into the international market is to look for international contacts in your local area. This will save you the cost of traveling to a foreign country and the frustration of dealing with language and cultural barriers.

The U.S. is truly a country of immigrants. We have the most diverse population on the planet. In any major city you can find people from many different countries. Particularly the countries mentioned earlier. For example, if your company were exporting into Japan, you could look for Japanese people—particularly businesspeople. Where might you find them? The international districts, exchange students in college, foreign language professors, interpreters, English as a second language teachers, import/export companies, foreign language clubs, and the airport.

If you plan to travel to a foreign country to recruit, here are a few suggestions. You might consider joining your local Rotary club and then write to a club in the country where you plan to travel. You can attend the meeting and make great contacts. In fact, quite often you may find a host who will provide housing and contacts while you are in the country.

One very successful distributor whose company was entering Taiwan, quit his job and went with a friend. Neither spoke Chinese or were familiar with the culture. They very quickly found English-speaking people who helped them find jobs and housing. They then utilized these contacts to find others and within a year had built huge networks.

The international markets offer huge potential, but don't forget what you have here in the U.S. There are 270 million people here in this country and only about 40 million are already involved in networking. That's a very big market and you never have to leave the country.

Chapter 6

Presentation

You Are the Messenger

The presentation is literally the foundation of your business. Many new network marketers think of their presentation as a sales pitch - you will be more successful if you think of it simply as sharing a message. The purpose of the presentation is not to sell prospects on network marketing, but rather to present the right information to enable them to make an educated decision. You are just the messenger. What they do with the information is up to them.

Despite the fact that the ultimate decision is up to the prospect, your presentation will make or break your business. I know one very successful distributor who studied his company for several months, then launched into three and four hour presentations. He told them everything he knew about network marketing, the products, and his company. Most of the prospects left with glazed eyes and never came back. The rest believed they couldn't be successful because they couldn't give a presentation that long. Needless to say, he didn't recruit many people until he shortened his presentation.

Your presentation should be short enough to keep your prospects' attention, and long enough to give them the basics and excitement of your business. An hour is the longest you will want to spend giving a presentation to a prospect. You should have a basic presentation that covers the essence of your business — an opener, a brief history or story about yourself and your company, the products, trends, compensation, training, and then a close. In preparation, you will need to study the company literature, listen to other successful distributors give presentations, and fill in the blanks by asking questions of your upline leaders. First, consider some different types of presentations.

Types of Presentations

Network marketers generally rely on nine different types of presentations, ranging from very brief, one- to two-minute presentations, group presentations, and, with current technology, computer online presentations. Each type of presentation will serve you in a different way as you build your network, and you will want to consider which you feel most comfortable using, and which are most effective to achieving your network goals.

"What Do You Do?"

A "What do you do?" presentation is a very brief presentation you can conduct either at business or social functions. Quite often people will ask you what you do for a living. This is your opportunity to create interest and a possible prospect. You should be prepared for a three- to five-minute version. For example, "I represent XYZ company. Are you familiar with them? They're one of the fastest growing businesses in the U.S. today. It's a debt-free company that has grown from a shoe-string start-up to over X million dollars a year in just X years. People have made a lot of money by helping other people. They're expanding into this area and are looking for some key leaders. Say, you might be able to help. Who do you know that might be interested in more money and more free time?"

One-on-One

You will use the one-on-one presentation the most. In this type of presentation, you meet with a prospect and cover all the basic points. Since you are alone with the prospect, you can tailor the presentation to the interest and personality type of the prospect. Some network marketing companies have flip charts or presentation books that you can use. The tendency of most network marketers is to talk at people, instead of with them. You want your presentation be a give and take conversation, so make sure you are asking questions throughout the presentation.

Two-on-One

If you have a good sponsor or upline, you should do many two-on-one presentations, particularly in the beginning. In this type of presentation, your sponsor or upline will do most of the talking, and you should watch and listen. Unless you have discussed your involvement in the presentation, it is a good idea for you to stay quiet. As you gain more knowledge and experience, you can handle larger parts of the presentation.

The two-on-one is a very effective way of presenting. Since there are two of you, you are less likely to miss some key details or be unable to answer a prospect's question. If you do a good job of involving the prospect, he or she will feel part of the team, rather than under attack.

Group Presentation or Opportunity Meeting

Most likely, you will not have to handle opportunity meetings for a while, unless no leaders are available to give them in your area. However, eventually you will want to become proficient at giving group presentations.

In this type of presentation, you cannot tailor to or get feedback from your prospects. An opportunity meeting is a more straightforward presentation. The key is to hit as many of your prospects' hot buttons as possible — issues that prospects care about and get excited about, such as financial or job security, personal challenge and growth, or other concerns you sense in your prospects. You want the presentation to be exciting, but not hypish. Most people get very turned off by hype. Don't jump up on the chairs and start shouting accolades of your company and products. You will have people running for the exits. Instead, just be honest and give them the facts with excitement in your voice.

Keep the presentation to 45 minutes or an hour in length. Attention starts to drift if you go beyond an hour. Just cover the basics. Don't try to give them everything at once.

Audio or Video Presentation

If you are fortunate enough to be with a company that has excellent opportunity presentation tapes, either audio or video, use them. Audio and video presentations are already done for you — what to include and exclude in a presentation has already been decided by the professionals who produced the tapes. Audio and video presentations can really leverage your time. How many hours would it take to give 20 presentations? At least 20 hours, plus set-up and clean-up time. How long would it take to mail out 20 audio or video tapes? — an hour at most. The audio or video tapes give the presentation exactly the same way every time — never a change in enthusiasm level, and nothing left out.

Don't rely totally on audio or video presentations. Combine them with some one-on-one or two-on-one presentations, as well as the group business briefings. Audio and video tapes are great for really busy people or people who are having trouble with the presentation. They are also great for long distance sponsoring.

Teleconference

A teleconference is nothing more than a group opportunity presentation over the phone. Check with your company to see if they currently offer teleconferences. If not, check the local telephone answering services to see if they offer a teleconferencing service and do your own.

You can conduct two types of teleconferences, an interactive one in which everyone can participate in the call, and a restricted one in which only the main speaker has audio access to the line. In a restricted call, all other connections allow listening only. If you are conducting purely an opportunity presentation, the restricted call is best. You won't have to fight the background sounds that are invariably created when you have a number of people involved in a call. On the other hand, if you are doing a training session or a product information call, you will want to use an interactive call so that people can ask questions and give testimonials. The interactive call also makes it easier to have additional experts on the line.

Many network marketing companies offer weekly national, and sometimes international teleconferences that you can tap into by calling the designated number and giving the code number. As with audio and video tapes, teleconferencing helps you leverage your time. You can call a prospect and have them listen in on the call right from their home. Then you can call afterwards and answer questions.

24-Hour Information Line

A 24-hour information line is either a local or 800 number that is answered by a voice mail system. You put on a short one- to two-minute message that really sells either the opportunity or the products. Prospects can call and listen to the message at any time.

Put your information number on advertisements, prospecting cards, brochures, and flyers, or just call prospects and tell them to listen to the information line. An information line is a great way to sift through large numbers of people to find those who are truly interested — another great way to leverage your time.

To set up a 24-hour information line, check with your parent company to see if they offer voice mail services. If not, look in the Yellow Pages under telephone — voice mail, just voice mail, or possibly telephone — answering. Find a company that offers independent voice mail boxes. They usually cost approximately $6 to $15 per month. Tell the voice mail company that you need an outgoing message time of at least two minutes. If possible, ask to test the voice mail box so you can see how easy or difficult it is to make and retrieve messages. Some systems are cumbersome and illogical, while others are very easy to use. Also, check voice quality of both your outgoing and incoming messages. Your information line will be totally ineffective if either your outgoing message or the incoming messages are garbled.

If you are setting up a new service, talk with the voice mail company about a program for your network. Get them to wave any set-up fees and discuss the possibility of a lower rate or a commission for you. Make sure their system will allow for intercommunications. That way you can send messages to all you distributors at once, instead of calling each box individually.

Fax-On-Demand

Fax-on-demand is a new service offered by AT&T and some of the more sophisticated fax/modem software systems for your personal computer. Fax-on-demand allows your prospects to call the fax-on-demand number, leave their fax number when prompted by the system, and then automatically receive a faxed information package. All the work is carried out by the computer — you do not have to do anything except prepare the information package that explains your business opportunity.

Include as a part of the information package an introductory letter, information on your company, a brief product or service description, a visual explanation of the compensation plan, starter packages, distributor agreement, product order form, and phone numbers to reach you and get more information, such as a 24-hour information line or teleconference number. Give instructions for completing the agreement and order form.

Since almost every office and many homes now have fax machines, a fax-on-demand number can be a great way to get information to people quickly. If you make a prospecting cold call and the prospect shows some interest, have him or her call (or you call) the fax-on-demand number, which will fax the information package immediately. Follow up the fax with a phone call an hour or two later. This system creates very quick turn around and is convenient for everyone.

Online Services and E-Mail

Computer online services such as Prodigy, Compuserve, America Online, and Internet all offer e-mail services. You can connect with other online users and pass messages through an electronic mail system. On some online systems you can get into interactive forums that allow direct communication between participants during certain times each day or week.

You can use online services in several ways. Some allow you to place classified ads to market either your opportunity or products. You can also use the e-mail system to send out an opportunity message. Those who respond would receive a full presentation in their e-mail box — for example, you might send the same presentation that you use in your fax-on-demand system. There are even mail box systems that will automatically e-mail an information packet when requested by a prospect online. You are then e-mailed the lead for follow-up.

With technological advances and the proliferation of home computer systems, eventually most network marketing activities will be accomplished through computer online services. People will communicate online and access your product catalog to order products directly from the parent company. Your company will provide updates and report on the growth in your network via online service. All training will occur in an online classroom. The time and cost savings potential of network marketing online is enormous.

As you develop your network marketing business, you should be prepared to use any of the presentation types described here. However, as you learn which are most effective for you, pick the two or three that you will use consistently. To decide which presentation types suit you, consider your strengths and weaknesses as a presenter.

You As a Presenter

Learning to be an effective presenter is critical to your long-term success in network marketing. Don't worry if you are not the best public speaker in the world. In fact, many of the top leaders in this industry were once terrible presenters.

Master Storyteller

The first key to an effective presentation is to become a master storyteller. People love to hear stories. A story causes the listener to get mentally involved. Begin with your own story — who approached you about network marketing and the company you represent? How did they approach you? How did you feel? What was your initial reaction? What research did you do? Why did you decide to get involved? What have been the benefits or results? How do you feel now? Why are you excited about this opportunity?

If your story isn't very interesting, talk to people upline from you — people who have probably been in network marketing longer — until you find someone who has a really interesting story. For example, one network marketer frequently tells the story of how his upline leader got into the business. This upline leader had once been a minister in an economically depressed town. His 1981 Chevy, with no hubcaps and a cracked windshield, was about to be repossessed and his small, one-bedroom house foreclosed. At that point, he was introduced to a network marketing company. At first he was very skeptical — in fact, he hated network marketing. But he was desperate, so he signed on as a distributor. Six months later he was earning $15,000 per month. He retired to Aspen, Colorado to write books and teach blind people how to ski. Due to the exponential growth of his network, seven years later he was earning over $100,000 per month.

Stories can help people really feel the emotion and excitement of turning one's financial fortunes around. A story like the one about the minister can show people that the American dream is still possible — to go from poor and destitute to financially stable as a result of one's own hard work. To inspire people to do the same for themselves is the goal of a good network marketing presentation. Work on your own stories and practice them until you are a master storyteller.

Know Your Stuff

It is important to have all your facts straight. Your prospects are already skeptical about network marketing, and if you don't know your material, their skepticism will grow. Study the company distributor manual and literature. Gather articles and information on network marketing and the product you sell. If you sell health and beauty aids, read as much as you can about the health and beauty industries. Facts and figures that you rattle off the top of your head will impress people. However, if you know and show too much knowledge, prospects may feel they can't do your business, because they would have to spend too much time studying. Give people just enough information to make an educated decision.

One of the most important areas you will need to know and answer questions about is the compensation plan. Prospects want to quickly understand how they can make money. Your job is to take what is usually a very complicated plan and melt it down to something that seems simple and easy to do. If your prospects can easily see how they can make money or achieve financial freedom, you have a good chance of sponsoring them. Study your company's compensation plan until you know it. Practice explaining it to other people, draw diagrams to illustrate, and show realistic examples. Paint a word picture of how distributors leverage their time, earning a monthly residual income, and creating financial wealth and the time freedom to really enjoy life. With practice, you will be able to present to prospects how network marketing compensation plans can work for them.

Internalize the Information

When you first start to give presentations don't be afraid to use crib notes. Put all the facts and figures on 3" x 5" cards and refer to them during your presentation. However, within a short period of time, you will want to have everything memorized and internalized — committed to memory and quickly available to you during a presentation.

An internalized presentation is one that, if your sponsor called you at 3:00 A.M, waking you out of a deep sleep, would be available to you without hesitation or flaw. By internalizing the information, you can then personalize it so that your presentation sounds very natural. Your prospects will be more attentive, impressed, and interested if your presentation sounds natural.

Be Enthusiastic

New distributors tend to have more enthusiasm than knowledge. Two or three years from now, your enthusiasm will have declined, but your knowledge will have increased. Chances are you will recruit more people in your first year than any other — due primarily to your level of enthusiasm.

If you are excited about your business, your prospects will feel the excitement and want to be a part of it. Enthusiasm and excitement sells. However, it must be genuine enthusiasm. You can't just act enthusiastic. In fact, if you are not enthusiastic about your opportunity, maybe it is the wrong one for you. Evaluate your enthusiasm level before you go on. Don't waste your time on an opportunity that doesn't excite you.

Ask Questions

As I mentioned earlier, many network marketers talk at their prospects. They can ramble off a full hour presentation without giving the prospect an opportunity to say a word. If you do this, your prospects may smile and nod, but then tell you they want to think about it — meaning, in fact, that they have no idea what you do and just want to get away from you.

Instead of spewing masses of information at your prospects, talk about one particular issue and then ask some questions to make sure you have their attention, understanding, and interest. Asking questions also gives prospects a chance to contribute to the presentation, to become involved and stay attentive. It also shows that you are interested in them.

The best type of questions to use in a presentation are confirming questions. These are questions that give you some feedback on prospects' understanding and interest level. Questions like, "Can you see why I am so excited?" or "Does that make sense?" are great confirming questions.

Practice making statements that end with a question. For example, you might say, "Our compensation plan has created total financial freedom for 50 people. Can you see how it could do that for you?" You can also use tiedown questions, such as "Isn't it, doesn't it, couldn't it, and wouldn't it?" You might say, "That's a tremendous product, isn't it?" A tie-down forces a prospect to pay attention and respond. It also helps you maintain control of the conversation by minimizing prospect questions that might take you off the main subject.

An old sales proverb says, "He who asks the most questions, wins." Get in the habit of asking questions during your presentation and you will experience much better results.

Keep the Prospect Involved

The more involved the prospect is in the presentation, the better your odds of signing a new distributor. As discussed in the last section, questions are a good way to maintain involvement, but questions alone are not enough.

You want the prospect both physically and mentally involved. To increase physical involvement, you can offer samples of your products or do a product demonstration. If possible, include the prospect in the demonstration. You can illustrate services, such as insurance or travel, with color pictures, graphs, charts, brochures, and catalogs. The prospect can hold them, examine them, and even take keep them to peruse later.

If you are a master storyteller, paint a word picture of what the prospect's life will be like after using your product or service or becoming a distributor. Get the prospect involved in a visualization exercise. Have prospects close their eyes and imagine themselves living in their dream home, having the free time to enjoy life, doing what they want every day, vacationing to exotic locations, buying the car of their dreams with cash, helping people who are less fortunate, sending the kids to college without borrowing money, helping their parents live a luxurious life in their golden years, never having to worry about money again! Get them feeling what it would be like. Once they see and feel it, their interest levels will increase dramatically.

Be A Good Listener

When you ask questions and engage your prospect in conversation during a presentation, you need to follow through by being a good listener. Internalizing the presentation becomes critical because if you are thinking about the next part of your presentation, you will have difficulty listening to your prospect and answering questions. If you have the information internalized, you can react quickly to questions or comments issued by the prospect.

We have two ears and one mouth because we are supposed to listen twice as much as we talk. If you concentrate on listening to your prospects, you will become a master network marketer, expand your network, and make money. Talking too much is the most common mistake made in network marketing. Telling the prospect about how great the products are and how people are making millions of dollars in the business will not convince a prospect. If you say it, they won't believe; if they say it, they will believe. Your job is to listen to what is important to the prospect and then help them say the right words.

You can be one of three different types of listeners:

- Active — you concentrate on hearing the words and seeing the body language to get the message.
- Reflective — you listen for the emotion or feelings and reflect them back to the speaker.
- Empathic — you listen for understanding of what the speaker really means.

Whether you are a good or poor listener, the way you listen is a habit you have developed over time — a habit you can change. For the next 21 days, practice being a good listener. Here are some tips:

- Concentrate on everything the person you are listening to says. Very often, people only listen to a portion of what is said and then spend the rest of the time composing a rebuttal. Unfortunately, the brain can only concentrate on one thing at a time, so you miss the rest of the message. When you hear only part of a person's message, your response will most likely be inappropriate.

- Listen completely rather than selectively to avoid selective hearing — hearing only what you want to hear.

- Listen rationally rather than emotionally. Stick to the facts and don't allow yourself to respond in an emotional manner. If you follow this advice, you will avoid jumping to incorrect conclusions, which result in misunderstandings, misinterpretation, and anger.

- Continue to listen completely, even if questions pop into your mind. These questions may get answered, but you will miss the answers if you are concentrating on these unanswered questions.

- When part of a group, take notes so you will remember the content later. Transferring your thoughts to paper requires you to concentrate on what is being said. If you think of a question, jot yourself a quick note so you will remember it later. Don't allow yourself to drift off on other thoughts. If you are taking notes, you give the speaker the indication that you are interested and listening. At the appropriate times, ask your questions.

- Listening indicates interest and intelligence. The best communicators are those who have mastered the skill of listening.

The best way to become a better listener is practice, practice, practice. When you are in social situations with groups of people, listen to each group until you have the gist of the conversation. Then ask some questions to show that you are an active listener. Reflect back to the speaker the feeling you get from his or her message and try to gain an understanding of the speaker's message and motivation.

It is said that people don't care how much you know until they know how much you care. Be a good listener. Get to know your prospects and their motivations, and let them know you care about them and their lives. Show them how your business can help them reach their life goals. Listening is the key.

Be Duplicatable

People who are highly successful in network marketing are easily duplicatable — the steps they take and strategies they use to build a successful network can by copied, adapted, and used by their distributors to build even bigger networks. For example, the poor minister who became a successful distributor gave his presentations in blue jeans and tennis shoes. He gave a brief introduction and then played a video tape. His prospects could see how they could easily duplicate his success. Consequently, he has nearly 30,000 distributors worldwide.

One network marketer was a professional and polished public speaker. When he gave a presentation, people raved about it, but no one would sign up. Finally, he realized that his prospects were intimidated by his skills as a presenter and felt they couldn't duplicate them. To solve this problem, he started using video tapes in his presentations — anyone can plug in a video tape — and in fact many more distributors signed up after he changed his presentation style.

Most network marketing companies are designed for easy duplication. Every distributor receives a kit, which usually contains training and marketing materials. Each new distributor starts with some consistency, and it is up to you to continue that consistency. Make sure all of your presentations are easily duplicatable.

Inviting Prospects to a Presentation

To be successful in network marketing, you will need to invite people to either attend a presentation or review presentation materials. A number of tremendous presenters have failed at network marketing because they couldn't invite. Inviting is a skill you must master and become comfortable with in order to reach high levels of success in network marketing.

Inviting People You Know

When inviting people you know — friends, family, business associates, old school mates — you need to bear in mind that you are offering them a gift. You are not trying to sell them or convince them to do something that isn't good for them. Network marketing has changed people's lives, allowing them to enjoy total financial and time freedom. You are offering the people you know the opportunity to secure their financial future and to free up their time so they can do what they want, instead of having to work all the time.

Once you have the proper mind set, you are ready to make the call. When calling someone you know and see often, start the conversation with the four concerns you probably share with everyone you know —family, occupation, recreation, and money, or the acronym FORM. As you proceed through these subjects, look for an opening to bring up your network marketing opportunity. Ask about the family and how they are doing. If you hear that they don't get enough time together, that is an opening. Ask about the job or business. If they bring up something negative, that's an opening to discuss the positives you have experienced as a network marketing distributor. Continue on to recreation by asking about upcoming vacations. If they don't have time for vacations, talk about the amount of free time you have as a network marketer. Money can be a difficult subject to bring up tactfully in casual conversation. You can mention something about the tough economy or the price of something you recently purchased. This will often stimulate a conversation.

Once you get an opening, launch right into your invitation. Say something like, "Sue, I've just recently encountered a very interesting financial opportunity. After carefully researching it, I feel like I'm going to make a bunch of money. Would you be interested in making some extra money?" Invariably they will ask what it is. Give them a good, but vague answer. You can use, for example, "It's a ten year old multi-national company that is going into a major growth phase that will take it from about $500 million to over $2 billion in the next five years. This is hot. We need to get together and look at this. How does (day) at (time) look to you?" If they don't have any questions and give you a favorable response, then set up an appointment or invite them to a presentation. However, if they give you any negatives, take away your invitation. Say something like, "On second thought, I'm not sure this is right for you. Let's just forget it." Sometimes when you take away the invitation or try to change the subject, the prospect calms down and accept the invitation.

Whether you get a negative or a positive response, make sure you ask for referrals. For example, you might say, "By the way, do you know anyone that might like to know about this fantastic opportunity?" Most often they will respond that they can't think of anyone. You may need to help them remember, by suggesting people, such as an insurance or real estate agent, business associate, or family member. If you get one referral, go for another. Try to get at least three.

Once a prospect has accepted your invitation, you need to assume a certain posture about the invitation. As discussed in Chapter 5 on prospecting, people who accept an invitation will sometimes do so without any intention of actually showing up. To increase the odds that the prospect will actually come to the presentation, set the appointment at their house or at a mutually agreed upon location, such as a restaurant that makes canceling difficult. This way they can't come up with a last minute excuse to cancel. If a real reason to cancel comes up, they can call the restaurant. Use the right words in confirming the appointment. "I know you said you will come, but I need to know that you will be there for sure. Timing is critical on this deal and we can't afford to waste any. Is there anything that would keep you from being there? I am talking with a number of people about this deal, so if you need to cancel, please give me at least 24-hour notice so I can put someone else in your spot." Confirming with posture will lend credibility to your network marketing program and increase your show-up percentage.

Another key to successful invitations is to sound confident over the phone. If you are tripping over your words, you create doubt in your prospect's mind. Write out a short script, like the one above. A good outline to follow is to use the four Cs:

- Compliment — Pay your prospect a compliment on something that relates to your business. For example, you might say, "You were always the most popular person in school." "You have tremendous people skills." "I've always admired your business abilities."

- Create Curiosity — Don't tell prospects too much over the phone. You want them to be curious. They ask questions because they are curious. If you answer them, the curiosity goes away. Refer to Chapter 5 on prospecting for more about how to create and maintain curiosity.

- Control — You need to maintain control of the conversation by asking questions. Each time you complete a statement, you need to ask a question.

- Commitment — Decide what you want out of the call, such as an appointment to come to a presentation or look at a video, and get a commitment.

All of the top network marketers use these strategies — FORM and the four Cs — to build their huge networks. If you use it, you will be amazed at the results.

Whatever you do, don't try to sell the opportunity over the phone. The more you try to sell it, the more prospects will back off. You feel that this is deceptive, but experience — by all successful network marketers — shows that you cannot best describe network marketing over the phone. People will only fully understand the industry and its potential when they can sit down with you in person, look at a video, and review your marketing materials.

Inviting People You Haven't Seen for Years

When you made your list of prospects in Chapter 5, you probably thought of people from high school, college, or a past job. Most likely, you haven't talked with these people in years. To call them up after such a long time might feel uncomfortable. However, you can handle the situation in a comfortable way. A good beginning is to say, "Larry, this is (your name) from high school. I'm calling you because we're looking for some business partners in your area and I thought of you. But first let's get caught up. Are you married?" Immediately ask questions about family, occupation, recreation, and money (FORM). After a few minutes of chit-chat, jump into your invitation.

The four Cs approach works very well with people you respected in high school. For example, you might say, "You were always the smartest (or most popular) kid in our class." Giving them a compliment right away will break the ice, and the rest of the conversation will be relatively easy.

Inviting People You Don't Know

As you read in Chapter 5, you will eventually run out of people you know and need to prospect in your cold market. The ratio of people called to those who attend a presentation will drop dramatically in the cold market, so you will need to talk with more people. However, there are over 270 million people in the United States and only about 15% of them are already involved in network marketing. That leaves you with approximately 230 million people. If you contact 30 each day, you would need 21,000 years to talk to all of them. Don't worry about not having enough prospects or the market getting saturated.

For long-term success, you will need to invite people you don't know to presentations. In Chapter 5, you read about all the different types of people you might prospect in your cold market, anyone from a referral, to a pizza delivery driver, to a person whose name you got from a business card. If you use advertising, some will be respondents to your ads. If you are really ambitious, you may even pick up the phone and start calling homes or businesses.

Your invitation to someone you don't know is going to be different than for people you know. Unless you have observed them or had some interaction, it will seem superficial to compliment them. You can approach a cold market invitation in different ways. Check with your sponsor or upline leader to see if they have developed a script that is working. If not, you might want to use the following. "Paul, this is (your name). Do you have a moment to talk? You don't know me, but your name came across my desk as a real professional in your field. I have your business card in front of me, it says that you work for (name of company). How long have you been with them? What do you like about working for them? Paul, I am a recruiter for a rapidly growing company. We are looking for some key leaders in this area. Our top people earn more each month than most people make in a year. Would you be interested in taking a look at our company?" They will always ask what company. "The name of the company is XYZ, have you heard of it?" When they say no, say "It is one of the hottest companies in the country. Why don't we set up an interview and I can get you some more information and answer all of your questions." If they are interested, they will set the appointment. If not, they will say no thank you. It is generally a waste of time to try and change their mind, so just move on.

As you prepare to prospect in your cold market, reread the section of Chapter 5 about how to secure referrals, business cards, or other references to people whom you might have success recruiting. Chapter 5 describes many different methods for prospecting people you do not know. If you can obtain names, business cards, or referrals, you will be more prepared to make the invitation.

The Network Marketer's Motto: Be Prepared

It is important that you never make a bad call. Many a new networker has fumbled and stumbled through their list of contacts. You don't want to burn these good contacts, so be prepared. Know what you are going to say, have a script in front of you, and practice and role play the call at least 20 times before starting your actual calls. Know what questions prospects will ask or objections they will throw out. Have the answers internalized.

If you are feeling tired, sick, or unenthusiastic, don't make any calls. Either pump yourself up and get on the phone with the right attitude, or take the day off from making prospecting calls. Keep in mind that the next call might yield your next leader.

The Enemy – Fear

If you are like most network marketers, you will constantly have to fight to keep fear from limiting your success. To become successful in network marketing, you will need to break through the fear barrier. Consider these methods for combatting fear:

- Remember that you have the gold mine and are offering it to this person. If they say no, you haven't lost anything.

- Figure out how much a new distributor is worth to you per year. Determine how many new contacts you need to make to secure a new distributor. Now figure out how much each contact is worth. If each contact is worth a $100, then whether they say yes, no, or maybe, you earned $100.

- The next person you contact just might help you become a millionaire. Mark Yarnell, a top network marketing distributor, contacted 200 people to get one distributor. That one distributor built a huge network of his own, from which Yarnell earns over $30,000 per month in bonuses. Was it worth it to get the 199 no's? What do you think?

- Turn your fear into excitement. The physiological reactions of fear and excitement are the same — butterflies in the stomach, perspiration, edginess, dry mouth. Since your body is going to experience the same things, why not view your fear as excitement?

- Just do it, over and over. After a while, the fear won't feel so bad.

If you want to be very successful in network marketing, you will need to become a master inviter. Everyone is always looking for the easy way out, but the reality is you need to present your opportunity to a lot of people to sponsor a big enough network to create financial freedom.

Parts of a Presentation

As you develop your presentation, you need to consider approximately eleven different elements, from your introductory remarks to product displays and handouts. The remainder of this chapter looks at each of these elements in detail and discusses how you can prepare your presentation for the best results.

Opener

During your opening remarks, you welcome the prospects and commend them for taking the time and having the courage to attend. Let them know you are here to share with them a business that has tremendous financial potential, a business that could literally change the rest of their lives and the lives of their families. Tell them to relax and take some notes. Assure them that there will be no pressure tactics and that what they will hear is the information necessary to make a decision about whether they want to pursue the business opportunity further. During the opener you must grab their attention. Be enthusiastic — if you are excited, they will be excited.

Your Story

After your opening remarks, go directly into your story. When you tell your story, you have a chance to brag about the success you have had as a network marketer and to lend credibility to the idea that this business opportunity will lead to financial freedom. Tell about your background, your family, job, or business, and why you chose network marketing as your avocation. Since prospects' primary objections are always money, time, sales, and skepticism about network marketing, cover these in this section.

Tell about how you were skeptical and that you did your research to prove that network marketing is not only legal, but an industry that is exploding worldwide. Quote current publications like *Success* magazine or other authoritative media that write positively about network marketing.

Talk about the limited time you had available before you started network marketing, that your job or business, family commitments, church or other social activities took up all your spare time. Then talk about how little extra time is necessary to build a network marketing business. Network marketing is the perfect vehicle for very busy people because it enables them to leverage their time by recruiting other people.

Discuss the amount of money people invest in franchises — an average of $45,000 just for the rights. People spend an average of $5,000 to start any other type of business. In most cases, a person can start a network marketing business for less than $100, plus a selection of products for their own use. Determine what figure you want to use and include it in your story.

The story portion of a presentation is also a good time to ease prospects' fears about sales. Describe your initial reaction to the similarity between network marketing and sales. Then discuss the principle of network marketing — distributors use great products and then share them with others. Describe how people often tell others about a great movie they saw. This kind of word-of-mouth advertising is network marketing, but these marketers don't get paid. Let your prospects know that they only need to do two things to be successful, share the products and share the opportunity — no sales involved.

Once you have told your story and described your personal feelings about network marketing, transition into the company story by describing how you were sponsored and what kind of research you did to make your decision.

The Company

In this part of your presentation, you need to build credibility for and interest in your company. Discuss the number of years the company has been in business. If the company is older than five years, talk about stability. If it has been operating for less than five years, talk about ground floor opportunity. Give prospects some insight into the founder of the company and the current management team. Talk about their abilities to build a giant company. Cover any facilities that the company owns, the computer system that will track the network, and the financial growth the company has experienced and will continue to enjoy in the future. Mention the mission of the company and what it is doing to make the world a better place to live. Talk security and long-term growth.

Products

Once you have described the company, introduce your prospects to the products. First, discuss the industry and how large it is. Talk about the projected future growth of the industry and what percentage your company is going to take. Then go into the basic philosophy behind your product line.

Discuss some of the best selling products in the line, and demonstrate one or two products if possible. However, don't show more than five individual products. More than five will overwhelm your prospects and takes too much time. Remember, in the presentation you are just giving them a good solid overview. Don't try to sell your whole line of products. Tell your prospects the name of the product, what it does for people, and the benefit if they were to use it. Discuss how it is different from anything they can buy at a standard retail store because it is of higher quality and better value. If you market a consumable product, you may want to give out samples. Get your prospects involved during this part of the presentation. Answer any questions they have about the products and then quickly move on.

Timing

Timing is very important in network marketing. Most people think it is best to sign on with a company when it is just starting up — on the ground floor. Often this is the toughest time for a network marketing company. It will have very few marketing materials and no track record. The best time to sign on with a network marketing company is when it has been in business for two to five years — before the first momentum growth phase, which starts at about $4 million per month.

When you talk about timing during your presentation, discuss where your company is in the growth cycle. Discuss the timing of your products in the marketplace. Also, explain how network marketing as an industry will go through its momentum growth phase during the next five to ten years.

Business analysts believe network marketing is where franchising was fifteen years ago — at the beginning of its momentum growth phase. Many also believe network marketing will be bigger than franchising. People who believed franchising would grow and bought franchises fifteen to twenty years ago are doing very well now. Tell people during your presentation that as network marketing begins its momentum growth, their networks will grow with it.

Trends

If any particular trends affect your company, be sure to discuss them in your presentation. For example, if you are marketing weight management or nutritional products, demonstrate to your prospects the proliferation of advertising and media coverage on those two subjects. Discuss the concerns people have about cancer, heart disease, diabetes, and aging, and how your company is addressing these issues.

You might also want to discuss the instability of the economy, the downsizing of corporate America, and forced early retirements, and tie these concerns into network marketing. Describe how network marketing can protect distributors from job insecurity.

You might also talk about how your company is positioned to sell to the baby boomer generation or generation X. For example, if your company sells products geared for people in retirement, talk about the aging of the enormous baby boomer generation and how it will sustain huge markets for products geared toward people in retirement. Many companies that have positioned themselves effectively for the changing demands of this huge baby boomer target market have become overnight successes.

If you know about natural market forces that are driving the growth of the industry and that of your company, be sure to discuss them in your presentation.

Compensation

Prospects will be very interested in knowing how compensation plans work. When you begin to describe them in your presentation, first show the differences between linear compensation and network marketing. A person can make money in four ways:

- Wages and salary — You can work for someone and get paid either a salary or an amount per hour; your income is limited by the time you spend at your job.
- Commission — You can work for someone or for yourself and earn a commission, giving you more flexibility, but still limiting the amount of work you can get done during each day.
- Investment — If you have money, you can invest it and use the leverage principal. In this case, the money you earn is not limited by time you can spend earning, but by the money you have to invest. Unfortunately, most people do not have a lot of extra money to invest.

- Time leverage — The fourth way to make money is to leverage your time, either by starting a company and hiring employees who do work for you, or by building a network of people who work for themselves and you get paid a royalty on the production they generate.

Network marketing is the best way to leverage your time and make money because it allows you to recruit a network of intelligent, hard-working people who go out and work for themselves every day. If you had a network of 1,000 people, and each one worked just one hour per day, that would be 1,000 work hours every day!

In your presentation, discuss the various ways a person can make money with your company. Show examples on a chalkboard, overhead projector, slide projector, or VCR. People need to see how they can make part-time and full-time money. In many states, you cannot mention the amounts of money top distributors make. If you can, do so. If not, then say things like, "Our top distributors earn more in a month than top corporate executives make in a year." If your company is a member of the Direct Selling Association (DSA), they may have figures on the average incomes of distributors in your company.

Do not go into too much detail or you will confuse your prospects, particularly those who have never seen or do not understand network marketing. Show them how they can make money retailing products, and discuss how they will be paid a residual income based on network distribution. Focus on the big picture, but be realistic or prospects will know that you are giving them hype rather than the facts.

Training and Support

Just about every network marketing company offers a distributor start-up kit. This usually includes a training manual, video and audio tapes, and company forms. No products should be included as this could be construed as front-loading, which was discussed in Chapter 1.

In your presentation, you want to describe the training materials that will come with their distributor kit and the cost of a kit. Discuss any training that is available through the company, either audio, video, or in-person training. Talk about how new distributors receive initial training and on-going support. Network marketing is a unique business in that people are in business for themselves, but not by themselves. Be sure to tell prospects that their success is dependent upon the success of others so that all distributors in a network work together and help each other succeed.

If you have some professional-looking training packages, show them to the prospects so they can see the quality of the training programs available. Talk about how simple network marketing is and let prospects know that they will have many mentors who will help them minimize the possibility of failure. But, also explain that in order to succeed they will need to work hard and follow the lead of these mentors.

Close

As part of your closing remarks, do a quick summary, such as, "All the pieces of the puzzle are here — the company, products, timing, compensation plan, training, and support. The only thing missing is you. At this point you are probably at one of three stages: 1) You are definitely interested in the business and want to know more; 2) You aren't interested in the business, but would like to try the products; or 3) You are not interested at all. If you are interested in knowing more about the business raise your hands. How about those interested in the products? Those two groups should stay for a few more minutes. The rest of you are welcome to leave at this point. We thank all of you for attending. We will stay after for as long as you like to answer questions. I want to leave you with one final thought. You are where you are today in your life because of decisions you made five years ago. Where you will be in five years will be determined by decisions you make today. We just hope you make the right one tonight. Thank you."

A standard presentation has all the elements described so far, opener, a story about yourself and your company, and a discussion about the products, timing, trends, compensation, and training and support. Check with your upline sponsor or leader to see if they have a standard presentation they prefer you to use. Write out your personal presentation and begin to memorize it. Practice with your spouse or upline. Make sure you are involving the prospects by asking questions or engaging them in activities. Keep the presentation under an hour. Work on projecting enthusiasm and excitement, and tape your presentation and listen to it. You may even want to take some speaking courses, join Toastmasters — there are chapters in every city — or buy books and tapes on public speaking. Always try to continue improving your presentation because it is vital to your success as a recruiter.

Product Display

Some network marketers like to use product displays in their presentations, arguing that they are an integral part of the presentation and allow for a natural transition at the end. Others say that, depending on the products, displays may scare people away or cause some preconceived ideas. For example if your company represents skin-care products and a man walks in for a presentation, he may immediately assume that the business is better suited for women. This is a preconceived idea that is incorrect or you would not have invited him.

You will have to experiment for yourself and discuss the pros and cons of product displays with your sponsor. If your products are attractively packaged, a product display can be a real asset. It gives the prospect a chance to see the product packaging, review ingredients or functions, and get a feel for the breadth of the product line. It also shows that you are proud of the products.

Depending on what kind of products you sell, the easiest way to set up a display is to purchase a small two- or three-shelf unit. Place your products on the shelves, using a creative arrangement. You may want to include some literature as part of the display.

Presentation Handouts

People retain more information if they receive it both orally and visually. Handouts can really reinforce the visual part of a presentation. However, don't pass out your handouts before or during your presentation because you will lose the audience immediately as they begin to read the handouts. Save handouts until the end and give them as a part of an information package.

Your information package could include literature, articles, audio or video tapes, and product samples. Give these packages to the people who seem very interested, but for whatever reason don't sign up. For the rest, make up a simple one-page flyer that restates the important points on both the products and opportunity.

The presentation is the heart of your business. It is where you will hook or lose potential distributors. If you do a good job of presenting, you will increase your close ratios and build a network much more quickly and reach your goals of financial and time freedom that much sooner.

Chapter 7

Objections, Closing, and Follow Up

Objections

Once you have developed a style and strategies for prospecting and presenting your opportunity, you will feel more comfortable with the process of building a network. However, no matter how successful you are, or how comfortable you feel with prospecting, you will always need to handle objections, close a presentation, and follow up. Succeeding with these three aspects of network marketing could make the difference in the size and success of your network marketing business.

Most people moan and groan when they hear the word objection. You may feel an objection is a rejection of you or a barrier to getting what you want. However, in network marketing, you will learn to love objections. They create an opportunity to continue a dialog.

Objections usually come in two forms. The first is a reactionary statement. Think about the last time you were in a department store and the sales clerk said, "Can I help you?" If you said, "No thank you, I'm just looking," that was a reactionary objection. You may have really needed a new shirt, had money in your pocket, and really needed help finding a certain size, but you still gave the clerk the objection. Perhaps you weren't ready for the clerk's help, you wanted more time to look around, or resented that the clerk thought you couldn't find the shirt yourself. The people you talk with will do the same thing and have some of the same feelings when they throw out reactionary objections.

The second type of objection is a request for more information. For example, some of your prospects will say, "I don't have the time."

What they are really saying is, "Show me how I could fit this into my busy schedule." Another common one that you will encounter is "I don't have any money." This typically means, "You haven't shown me enough value to warrant finding the money." You need to interpret the objections, find the hidden question, and answer it.

Why do prospects object? It's human nature. We have been programmed to say no, but we don't like saying no, so we come up with an excuse. People don't like to say no, so you have to show them enough value in your program to illicit a yes.

Most Common Objections

Some of the most common objections in network marketing include:

- "Is this one of those pyramid schemes?"
- "I wouldn't be interested."
- "I don't have the time."
- "I don't have the money."
- "I don't know many people."
- "I can't sell."
- "I've never run a business before."
- "I don't want to jeopardize my job."
- "I can't see myself doing that."
- "I'd lose all my friends."
- "I'd lose my status."

The last two types of objections, "I'd lose all my friends," and "I'd lose my status," are usually unspoken. People fear that prospecting their friends or pursuing with a type of business that receives some negative publicity would jeopardize their friendships and their status in society or the business world. These may be the most difficult types of objections, that you have to handle.

Handling Objections

Every type of network marketing business has a little different way to handle the various types of objections, so check with your sponsor or upline leader to see if they have answers. However, you can generally rely on the following six-step approach to handling all types of objections.

- Listen — Listen to the entire objection. Most often, people will hear the first couple of words and begin to think of an answer. I have seen prospects go full circle and answer their own objection. If you are not listening, you could look pretty stupid.

- Restate the objection in your own words — For example, you might say, "If I understand what you are saying, you don't feel you could fit another activity into your busy schedule. Is that correct?" Restating the objection shows that you were listening, allows you to clarify the objection, and allows the prospect to either answer his or her own objection or disregard it as unimportant.

- Agree or show understanding — By saying, "I understand how you feel," "I can see how you might feel that way," or "When people look at this for the first time, they often feel as you do," you empathize with the prospect, and open room for dialog.

- Answer — You can answer an objection in many ways. The most logical, but usually least effective, is verbally. The best way to answer an objection is to combine a verbal answer with visual reinforcement, such as articles, charts, graphs, and testimonial letters. People tend to disbelieve what they hear and believe what they see, so show them the proof. *Success* magazine has published numerous positive articles about network marketing. You can also find several books about the growth and viability of network marketing. All of these will help answer a prospect's objection.

- Confirmation — Make sure that you have answered the objection to the satisfaction of your prospect. Ask, "Does that answer your question?" or "have we covered that to your satisfaction?"

- Close — Once you have confirmed the answer, ask a closing question that gives two or three positive options. For example, you might ask, "Would you like to start with the small product sampler or the full line package?"

This six-step approach works wonderfully, if you actually use it. Most network marketers read all the books and listen to all the tapes, but never internalize the information. You can opt for rejection, or you can practice and use a system of answering objections that works.

One final hint regarding objections — if they give you too many, do not try to answer them all. Move on to the next prospect. People who give you objection after objection are too skeptical for this business.

Closing

To sell products and sign-up new distributors, you need to close. What is closing? It is simply asking prospects if they want to buy or sign up. Generally, if you don't ask, they won't buy or get involved. Closing can be a problem for network marketers because they haven't had any sales training. However, you do not have to be a polished salesperson to successfully close. Closing is not some mysterious secret. In fact the simpler you make your closes, the easier they will be, and the more duplicatable you will be. This section discusses three closes that work well and have been used by some of the top people in the industry.

The Million Dollar Close

The gentleman who developed this sophisticated technique is one of the best recruiters in network marketing. During his first three years in network marketing, he averaged over 60 new distributors per year. He now has a network of more than 15,000 people worldwide and earns more than $200,000 per month.

The million dollar close is probably the simplest technique you can use, yet it rarely occurs to network marketers that closing can be this simple. After a complete presentation, simply ask "What do you think?" It is simple and duplicatable. You and your downline distributors do not have to be veteran salespeople to use this close. In fact, you don't even have to have a good memory. Just remember four simple words that have generated millions of dollars of income for distributors all across the country, "What do you think?"

The Alternate of Choice

Despite the simplicity of the million dollar close, you can adopt others that work just as well. A type of close that has worked successfully for many network marketers is the alternate of choice, a close that uses two positive alternatives. The prospect cannot say no. For example, if you are calling for an appointment, you might say, "Would you like to meet on Thursday at noon or Friday at 3:00?" To answer the question, the prospect must pick one of the two alternatives, or come up with an objection, which you learned how to handle in the previous section.

You can use the alternate of choice for many different purposes. If you were discussing products, you could say, "Did you want the basic or deluxe model?" For closing on the opportunity, you might say, "Are you interested in making a little extra money, or do you want to go for financial freedom?" In fact, you could use this technique in your personal life. If you have children who avoid their chores, you might say, "Would you like to clean your room or take out the garbage first?" The alternate of choice is easy to use and generates quick decisions.

Triplicate of Choice

The triplicate of choice works like the alternate of choice, except you offer the prospect three positive choices. Like the alternate of choice it gives the prospect only positive options. The triplicate of choice works best if you have pre-planned and practiced so that it sounds natural.

The best way to implement the triplicate of choice is to give the prospect three different investment options, from low to high. The first choice should be the budget version. The second is the most common selection. The third is the high investment version that is actually the best selection for the prospect and is the highest priced, too. For example, a very effective triplicate of choice close is:

> "There are three ways to get started in my business. The first is our budget package. This is for the person on a strict budget, who can't afford much, but wants to get started. The second choice is our most common package. It contains all the things you need to operate a business. The third option is actually the best package, but it is only for the real achievers. Which of the three packages best fits your needs?"

If you write an effective three package close and practice it until it is natural, it can be very powerful.

Trial Closes

Closing is like a game. Every little yes you get moves you closer to the big yes — an agreement from a prospect to become a distributor.

Trial closes are questions that illicit little yes's. For example, if you market nutrition products, after discussing the products with the prospect, you might say, "Can you see how millions of people could benefit from these products?" If you sell water filters, you might have the prospect taste filtered and unfiltered water and then say, "Can you taste the difference?" Most likely, a prospect will answer yes to these questions, and you should capitalize on these yes's as signs that the prospect's interest in the products and the opportunity is increasing.

You can use trial closes every time you make a statement. By asking a question after a statement, you maintain control of the conversation. For example, you might say, "According to the Social Security Administration, only one out of every 100 people between the ages of 25 and 65 will be wealthy. Wouldn't you like to be that one?" This works very well on prospecting calls. Prospects tend to want to ask a lot of questions. By making statements followed with a question, prospects will answer the questions instead of ask them, and you will maintain control of the conversation.

A great way to trial close is to use the tie downs introduced in Chapter 6. A tie down is a natural question that is added to a statement. For example, "These products are very beneficial, aren't they?" "You would like to secure your financial future, wouldn't you?" or "This business could really change your future, couldn't it?" You can see how tie downs could be very valuable closing tools, can't you? That was a tie down, wasn't it?

Closing is not pushing people or forcing people to do things they don't want to do. Rather, it is guiding them into a decision that is good for them. If you come to realize that the decision is not good for a prospect, don't ask the question. Closing as an integral part of every interaction with a prospect, and you will soon master the technique and help introduce prospects to the financial opportunity that benefits them.

Follow Up

The goal of follow up is to check in with prospects who do not respond initially to a presentation, but who might respond more favorably as they are given time to think about the opportunity or products, or whose life situations may change.

Follow up starts with a mental process. You have to prepare every prospect for the follow up. Make sure prospects feel comfortable with the idea that they do not need to sign up that day. Do everything you can to get prospects signed up, but if you can't, rely on your follow-up system to reintroduce them to the opportunity later.

Your System

The first part of effective follow up is to have a system. If you have a computer, a simple database program will do. While a computer data base is very efficient, it is not very duplicatable. Until everyone has a computer in their home, you will need to consider a manual follow-up system.

One of the best manual systems uses a 3" 3-ring binder, alphabetical tab, A-Z, month tabs, January – December, and day tabs, 1 – 31. Make up a prospect information sheet with name, address, phone numbers, spouses name, number of children and names, birthdays, anniversary date, occupations, hobbies, primary interest in business, other comments, and some room for future contacts. Place these completed sheets in the alphabetical section. After the alphabetical section, place the current month tab, followed by the 1 – 31 tabs. After each contact with a prospect, set a follow-up date and write their name and phone number under that particular day, if during the current month, or behind the appropriate month, if during a future month. Each day, check the appropriate tab to see who you need to follow up with — the tabs serve as reminders, or ticklers, that you should follow up with someone that day. This follow-up system works very well for many network marketers.

Once you have a data storage and tickler system, the next step is to gather the information to put into the system. Have your follow-up system with you always. Whenever you meet with a new prospect, complete a prospect information sheet and enter it immediately into your system. Don't allow them to stack up or you will lose some of your prospects. Each day, as you are planning your time, review the contacts for that day in the 1 – 31 section. If you get in the habits of entering the information immediately and checking it daily, you won't miss future contacts.

Methods

The last part of an effective follow-up system is to determine the methods of contact. You will want to mix telephone, mail, and in-person contacts. Develop a selection of mailable pieces, such as news articles, booklets, postcards, thank you notes, letters, mailers, and newsletters. Establish a schedule for recontacting your prospects. How often will you call, mail something, or actually see them?

Never just call to see if the prospect is now ready to sign up. Have a new and exciting reason to call. Call to give the prospect new information, to set up a three-way call with a successful upline or a conference call with top distributors, or to describe some new products. These are all good reasons to contact. Contact by telephone every 30 days.

Try to have face-to-face contact with your prospects at least quarterly. Invite them to a business briefing, a product demonstration, or maybe an unrelated business seminar. Breakfast, coffee, lunch, or dinner are good choices. Invite them to come meet someone, such as your upline leader or a guest speaker who is in town.

Mailing is very time efficient, but is easily discarded. Mail something to prospects at least once a month. Hot prospects should get two or three mailings each month, so have a good selection of mailable materials. Check with your upline and the company for mailers. Develop some quick and simple postcards. If you have a computer and the time, create a monthly, bi-monthly, or quarterly newsletter. Newsletters are read more often and produce better results than other types of promotional mailers.

A powerful mailer is the thank you note. Go to a local print shop and ask them if they carry or have access to business thank you notes or order them from Execards, 300 North Valley Dr., Grants Pass, OR 97526. An appropriate business thank you note is typically 5½" x 8" before folding. They have Thank You stamped or printed on the out-side panel and business card slots on the inside. Write your own hand written note — it has more impact than pre-printed notes. Thank you notes are very powerful. Don't overlook them.

News articles are perfect mailers for sending prospects new informa-tion. Try subscribing to *Success* magazine so that you will have the monthly articles it publishes on network marketing. If your budget allows, subscribe to *Inc.* and *Entrepreneur* as well. Review these mag-azines each month for articles on network marketing, corporate down-sizing, entrepreneurship, starting or operating a small business, the baby boomers, unemployment, and retirement — anything that would be of interest to your prospects and might help them see the big pic-ture a little better.

Upline, a high-quality newsletter for the network marketing industry, is excellent for articles specifically about network marketing. *Upline* is located at 400 East Jefferson, Charlottesville, Virginia 22902. The *Highlander Club* newsletter is another good source of information on network marketing. They are located at Inner Harbor, 211 E. Lombard St. #368, Baltimore, MD 21202.

Try also your local newspaper, the *Wall Street Journal*, and *USA Today*. Keep your eyes and ears open for articles, cut them out, make a number of copies, and keep them in a file folder. These are great mailers for your follow-up system.

Keep track of what you have mailed to your prospects in your follow-up system. After your mailing, call each prospect to see if they received it. A follow-up call gives you a chance for another contact and to assess the prospect's current attitude about network marketing to see if anything has changed.

Retail Follow Up

In addition to following up with potential distributors, you also need to follow up with customers. While your product may be so good that it will sell itself, you should still try to help it along. Each time you get new customers, immediately send them a thank you note with a gift certificate good for $5 or $10 worth of your products on their next order. Estimate the time it takes a customer to use up the product and set your customers up on a calling schedule. Never call just to find out if they are going to buy something. Have some new information or a new product to introduce. Announcing a monthly special creates a great opportunity to follow up with customers.

Most network marketers who fail do so because they neglect to follow up effectively. They expect people to flock to them and then to collect the big bonus check. The reality is that you have to go to the people, again and again. Be persistent without being obnoxious. An effective follow-up program is the key.

When you become skilled at handling objections, closing, and following up, your network will begin to grow. As it grows, you will sign up more and more distributors. The sign-up procedure is as important to your overall success as any of the steps discussed so far. Chapter 8 discusses the sign-up procedure in some detail.

The Sign-Up Procedure

Why Is the Sign Up Procedure So Important?

Although this is a short chapter, it may be the most critical to your long-term success. Many network marketers who are recruiting maniacs, recruiting 10 to 20 people per month by bullying them to buy a start-up kit lose their distributors because the prospects really didn't have a good reason to get into network marketing. Your job, as a professional network marketer, is to find people who are ready for this business and help them get started the right way.

You never want to convince someone they should become a network marketer. A prospect has to believe in this business first before he or she can really commit to being and staying involved.

The way in which you sign up a new distributor will dictate his or her level of success. Since this is a business of duplication, if you sign them up incorrectly, they will have limited success, and so will the rest of your network. On the other hand, if you sign prospects up correctly, they will achieve higher levels of success, and that will duplicate all through your network.

Check with your upline to see if there are standard sign-up procedures. If not, then use the information that follows, which some of the most successful network marketers use in their businesses.

From Skepticism to Excitement

People don't wake up one day and decide to go into network marketing. They are contacted either by someone they know or don't know and introduced to the industry and to a particular company. Since they weren't prepared for it, they are skeptical and cautious. It is only during the sign-up procedure that much of this tension can be released and the prospect, now a new distributor, can get excited and begin to see glimpses of the potential success.

Consider two typical network marketing examples. John is a sales representative for a copier company. His wife Sue is a third grade teacher. They make a good amount of money and would like to buy a house within the next year. Paul, a business associate of John's, approaches him with the idea of creating a residual income that would allow them to buy the house. John is interested. Sue is very skeptical. She's heard about those pyramid schemes. But John persuades her to attend an opportunity meeting. The speaker is from out of town, one of the top money earners in the company. John and Sue are impressed. Paul shows them a distributor kit and tells them they have nothing to lose by signing up tonight. John and Sue would rather think about it. Paul's sponsor joins in and begins to press John and Sue to join right then. He's smooth and good, handling every objection they throw out. Finally, they give up and write a check for a distributor kit.

On the way home, John and Sue talk about how great the company and products seem, but aren't sure they could pressure people into business like Paul and his sponsor did. Plus, they have never operated a business, so that scares them. What do they do first? How do they get started? They begin to doubt that they can be successful. By the time they get home, they are convinced that they've made a mistake. Not wanting to hurt Paul's feelings, they decide not to return the kit.

A couple of days later, Paul talks with John about how things are going. John says that he's just been too busy to get started, but hopes to have time soon. Paul is excited that John is in his network. He knows that John and Sue are going to be big hitters and make him a lot of money. Paul tells John that if he needs anything to call.

John is just stringing Paul along. He and Sue have no intention of doing anything. Odds are they will never even buy any products. They will become zeros on Paul's network printout, and he will probably never understand why.

Now consider a second scenario. Tom and Jill are out to dinner with their friends Bill and Paula. In the conversation Tom happens to mention that he isn't happy with his job. Bill mentions that he and Paula have recently started a business that might be of interest to Tom and Jill. Paula suggests that they attend a business briefing on Thursday evening. Tom and Jill accept.

When Tom and Jill arrive at the hotel, they are greeted by Paula, who takes them to meet the guest speaker. Paula explains that she is one of the top money earners in the company. Tom and Jill find her to be a very caring and likable person. Tom and Jill are very impressed. After the presentation, Bill and Paula answer some questions and discuss the start-up procedure with Tom and Jill. Tom is a little skeptical because he has heard about these pyramid schemes. But Paula is able to clear that up quickly with a brochure from the attorney general's office that discusses the difference between legal network marketing companies and illegal pyramid schemes. Bill asks if they have any additional questions, and then asks if they would like to become distributors. Tom says that they would like to discuss it and then make a decision. Paula tells them that is smart. They should research and make a good decision. However, timing is also important, and every day that they are not building their business is a day forever lost. Bill gives them a professional looking information packet and says that he will give them a call the next evening to answer any questions.

On the ride home, Jill starts to thumb through the materials and comments on how impressive they look. Tom indicates that he was impressed with everything about the company and that it seems like a good opportunity. When they arrive home, they spend some time looking through the materials. They talk about how they could work at the business part-time and generate some extra income. Then they could work toward replacing Tom's income, so he could quit his job and build their business full-time. Neither Tom nor Jill sleep very well that night. They have network marketing fever.

The next night when Bill calls, Tom says that they are very interested and want to meet right away. When they meet, Bill explains what it will take to be successful. They must order some products, try them out and see what good quality they are. They must commit to attending a meeting every week. They must commit to following the marketing program exactly and not try to recreate the wheel. Most of all, they must make a commitment of at least one year. Tom and Jill agree. Paula walks them through the starter kit and distributor agreement. They complete the agreement and a product order form, with some products for their own use and some to retail. Tom and Jill are very excited and want to start calling people. Bill cautions them to wait until they have gone through the training. He warns them that a few rejections from prospects could destroy their excitement about the business. Paula gives Tom and Jill some assignments and they set an appointment for the initial training two days later. Bill demonstrates a prospecting call by calling Tom and Jill's top five potential prospects. Bill uses a referral approach. Tom and Jill listen in, but don't participate in the call. Bill sets three appointments.

Tom and Jill leave excited and motivated. This is going to be a great business and they have a great upline team in Bill and Paula. This training and assistance is what network marketing is all about, people helping people reach their goals.

It is easy to see the differences in these two examples. These were both real life scenarios, and the sign-up procedure made the difference between a zero and a very excited distributor. How important is the sign-up procedure? It is critical to your long-term success.

The Start-Up Procedure

The most important factor in the start-up procedure is your attitude. If you are just trying to sign people up, the advice here will not help you. If you are really interested in the success of your new distributors, then you will see greater success.

The following 15-step process will assure that you have successful start ups and a successful network.

1. Confirmation and reassurance —The decision to start a business is a tough one. Make sure that you help your prospects with the decision by summarizing the benefits to new distributors and reassuring them that they have made a good decision.

2. Distributor kit — Next, go over the distributor kit and answer any questions. Discuss how distributors order products, complete a distributor agreement and a product order form or receipt, if you are supplying the products at retail.

3. Dream session — As discussed in Chapter 2 on success principles, it is important in network marketing to set goals, including dream goals. Once a prospect becomes interested and orders the products, you want to show him or her how to set dream goals. Help your prospect visualize a time in the future when money and time are no longer an object, when they could have, do, or be anything, go anywhere, meet anyone. Have the prospect individually write their dreams for five minutes. What would they buy? Where would they travel? Who would they meet? If you are working with partners, such as a husband and wife, have them compare their lists. This is fun, because they will usually discover things they didn't know about each others dreams. You will want to write down some of the dreams that seem to be most important for both of them in case you need to motivate them later on by reminding them of their dream goals.

4. 30-day goals — Once your future distributor has thought about some dream goals, help them work out some short-term goals. A good bench mark for setting goals is around 30 days. Some 30-day goals might include number of products used, number of retail customers, number of prospective distributors contacted, first business preview, first product demonstration, or first bonus check. By helping prospects set a short-term goal during the start up, you give them direction and something you can work on together during the training period. Make sure you have a copy of their 30-day goals.

5. Product order — Help your new distributor place their first product order for personal use and to retail. Make sure you include sales aids, such as brochures, catalogs, tapes, and samples. You should base this order somewhat on their goals. If they have a pretty large 30-day goal, they may need more products or marketing materials. If you have a standard start-up product package on hand, show them how to complete a product order form, but just supply the product out of your inventory. Network marketers debate whether

you should sell products to new distributors at wholesale or retail prices. Choose the method and price you feel comfortable with, or what your sponsor recommends, but in the end it doesn't matter as long as the new distributor has the products to use.

6. Read, listen, watch — Give your new distributor an assignment to read, listen, and watch all materials in the distributor kit. Ask them to make up a list of questions to be answered at the initial training session.

7. Use the products — If you have supplied your new distributor with a product kit, encourage them to use all of the products prior to the initial training so they can ask questions and give feedback.

8. Commit to a meeting schedule — Weekly meetings keep people excited and motivated. No successful network marketers fail to attend a weekly meeting. Make sure your new distributors attend meetings so that they can stay motivated and continue to learn to techniques and trends.

9. List of prospects — Ask your new distributor to develop a list of 100 prospects by the initial training session, which should occur two days after the sign up. Remind them not to pre-qualify people.

10. List of questions — As your new distributor is reading, listening, and watching the training materials, have them write down any questions that pop up.

11. One-year goal — Have your new distributor write a one year goal. The best type of one-year goal is an income goal, such as "It is now (date) and I am earning (amount) per month from my network marketing business."

12. Time commitment — Ask your new distributor to analyze their typical week and commit to a certain number of hours each week to working on the business. Have them mark those hours on a calendar, such as, 5:00 to 9:00 P.M. on Monday, Tuesday, Wednesday; 10:00 A.M. to 12:00 noon on Saturday.

13. Dreamstealers — Warn your new distributor about the people in their life who will try to steal their dream of financial and time freedom. Explain that these people could be family, friends, or business associates. They mean well, but just don't have enough

information to understand. Tell them to listen politely, but disregard anything they say about your company, products, or industry.

14. Three-way calls — There is no better way to start a new distributor than by helping them get new business. Ask them for the names of five really good prospects. Get on the phone and call them with your prospect listening in. You handle the complete call. Out of five calls, you will probably get two or three appointments. Your distributor will leave with a great feeling about this business. When someone tries to tell your new distributor that network marketing doesn't work because no one wants to hear about it, your new distributor can respond with three appointments in their first day.

15. Appointment for initial training — Set a date and time for the initial training. This appointment should be no later than two days from the sign-up date.

After your new distributor has written all the assignments and you have set the appointment for the first training, ask if they have any additional questions. Re-affirm the decision to start their own business and join your company. Let them know that you will be calling every day for the next 30 days to see how you can help them. Establish the best time for your call. Send them on their way, knowing you have done the best job of getting them started in network marketing.

To continue your job as a sponsor, you will lead your new distributors through training sessions, and continue your sponsorship with follow-up support. Chapter 9 describes the kinds of training and support that are available in network marketing.

Training and Support

Allay Common Fears

Providing excellent training and support for your new distributors is extremely important to the overall success of your network — which is what brings in bonus checks for you. One of the biggest fears in starting a new business is the fear of not knowing whether the business will succeed. A solid training and support program will alleviate many of your distributors' fears right from the beginning. Effective distributor training will cement your success in network marketing.

Check with your sponsor and upline to see if they use a consistent training program. If you have a successful upline, use their program. Otherwise, adapt the training program described in this chapter to the needs of your network. This program was developed by John Kalench, a very successful network marketing distributor, consultant, and author, and fine-tuned through use by many of the top distributors.

Build a Solid Training and Support Program

Training needs to be carefully organized. As with presentations, you cannot just improvise. The program should also be interactive, not dictatorial. Don't just tell your new distributor what to do. A program that enables you to help your new distributor discover things makes for interactive learning, which is the most powerful type of learning. When new distributors are involved in the learning process, they will remember and believe more.

The training program outlined here has three parts, psychology, product, and business. Each is critical to the training, and each part builds on the last.

Psychology

Network marketing has different challenges and requires a different kind of commitment than other businesses. Hard work over one- to three-years can turn a poor person into a millionaire, all for an investment of under $100. What other business has that potential? Unfortunately, the small initial investment and the high potential return of network marketing creates skeptics out of most people. Many high-powered businesspeople do not take network marketing seriously.

For example, if you decide to start your own business and you research the market, you will discover four options: start from scratch, buy a business, buy a franchise, and network marketing. Starting a business from scratch, buying a business or franchise required a person to have money to invest. Starting a business and buying an existing business also requires expertise in that kind of business, which is not required in franchising or networking. In these types of businesses you receive training and have mentors who work with you. So generally the choices boil down to franchising or network marketing.

Franchises have some very large start-up costs, usually $100,000 in franchise fees, plus capitalization of $500,000 for a building, equipment, and supplies. Once your business is operational, you will probably work 12- to 18-hour days for the first couple of years, with an average annual income of $100,000 or less.

In the network marketing option, your investment is usually under $100, and you will start working part-time, 10 to 15 hours per week. Within a year, you may be able to replace your employment income and begin working your network marketing business full-time. Within two to five years, you have the potential to make more in a month than most people make in a year. Once you build your network, your income will be a walk-away residual income — if you become disabled or just decide to retire, your income from bonuses on your network will continue.

Most people choose, when faced with these two options, the franchise because it seems more like a traditional business. Network marketing doesn't seem real to most people. Therefore, the first step in the training process is to help new distributors believe that network marketing is a legitimate, viable business.

You will need to discuss some key issues. Every prospect wants to know that the business is simple, that it is fun, that they can make money, that the timing is perfect for them now, and that they will receive training and support.

One of the best ways to build belief is through examples. As a part of your training package, put together written, audio, and video testimonials from successful people in your business. If your company or upline does not already have them available, then contact top distributors and make your own. Once you have a finished product, you may be able to market it through your company for the benefit of other distributors.

New distributors need to know that people just like them have become successful. Your testimonials should cover the gamut of situations — people with various backgrounds and financial situations, people who were poor and desolate, successful corporate executives, homemakers, doctors, dentists, ministers, lawyers, professional sports figures, politicians, and laborers. Somewhere among all those people, your new distributor will find someone to associate with, lending credibility to the network marketing industry.

To help your new distributors believe in their new business, you need to show them that the products are really good, that the company can deliver on time, that checks come out on time, that people actually buy the products and sign-up as distributors. Quite often, attending a company convention or seeing the company facilities can make a big difference in how your distributors view the company and the industry as a whole.

You can have the greatest products and opportunity in the world, but if your new distributors don't develop a strong belief in the viability and growth of the business, they will quit at the first negative. Make sure you spend at least 20 minutes of the initial training on your distributor's attitude toward and feelings about network marketing, and continue to work on distributors' belief in the business at every opportunity.

Products

The best way to learn about your products is to use them. You must teach your new distributor to be a product of the product. Once they see benefits from the products, they will begin telling other people about them. To increase a new distributors' knowledge of the products, make up a product benefit worksheet. On this sheet, list the different products and the benefits that you, your family, and your customers have enjoyed. Get together with other distributors and get their feedback on the products as well. Be sure to discuss the benefits of the product, not the features. Features have to do with the product, such as special ingredients. Benefits are what the product does for people, such as more energy, softer skin, better tasting water, or a safer home.

The next step in educating your distributors about the product is to discuss the company literature. Distributors do not need to be technical experts. A very successful distributor for a company that sells skin care products always comments about how he doesn't know what's in the products or why they work. He just knows that they do work. Besides, most people get involved in network marketing to make money, not to use products. Distributors want financial and time freedom, so don't worry if you don't know all the ingredients or why the products work. Just know that they do.

Next, work with the distributor on who is most likely to use the products. Every product has a target market — the people who are best suited to use the products. People in your target market have a need for your product, the money to purchase it, and are easily accessible to you. Talk about some of the people the distributor knows who fit into these categories. Make up a product prospect list and identify the products that the distributor should shared with each one.

Discuss the most common product questions. Prepare a handout for the distributor with these common product questions and various answers to them. Talk about product questions that the distributor has and add them to the list. Give the question and answer sheet to the distributor and do some role playing. You play the customer and ask the new distributor questions about the products. Role play helps the distributor become more comfortable with answering questions.

Next, discuss how to market the products. Refer again to Chapter 4 on retailing for some excellent marketing techniques. Spend an hour educating and training your distributor on how to use, market, and sell products.

Business

Spend the final part of your training covering the operations of the distributor's network marketing business. You can generally break this portion of the training into five parts, industry, company, compensation plan, prospecting and recruiting, and training and support.

Understanding the network marketing industry is critical to success. Many people do not understand it and try to discredit it as a scam or scheme. Your new distributors will quickly encounter this kind of negative feedback in their network marketing career. They need to have a good feeling about the industry.

Start your business training by showing them some positive literature about network marketing, such as the *Success* magazine articles. Talk about how network marketing is similar to franchising, how franchising was considered to be a scam in the 1950s, but now contributes more than one-third of the U.S. gross national product. Talk about how network marketing capitalizes on current social trends, such as home shopping and home-based business. Discuss the potential growth of network marketing in the United States — 270 million people living in the United States and only 40 million are involved in the direct selling industry. Direct selling is expected to grow enormously in the next decade.

Let them know that network marketing is big in other parts of the world, too. More network marketing is conducted in Japan than in the United States. In fact, Asian countries are much more network oriented than the United States. Companies like Amway and NuSkin have done very well in the international markets. With the NAFTA agreement, Canada and Mexico will become even bigger networking markets.

Paint a picture of the future — billions of people worldwide all hooked into huge networks by computer. They will buy and sell products, prospect and recruit, train and support their networks via computer online services, probably provided by a network marketing company. Very few people will not be involved in a network. The cream of society will be those who have the largest networks. There will be two classes of people — those with networks and those without. People with established networks will enjoy more time freedom, and the leisure industry will explode — with leisure activities and products of course offered through network marketing companies. To take part in this exploding trend, it is important to develop a big network now.

Next, discuss your company and why it is the best. Remember to give the new distributor just what they will need to train their new distributors. Don't overload them with useless information. Key topics to discuss include:

- When the company started;
- Who the principals are;
- What the financial status, facilities, and stature of the company in the industry is; and
- The company's timing and growth statistics.

Your new distributors will encounter thousands of network marketing companies and they need to understand why their company is the best. Knowing the facts about the company will help distributors when they talk to prospects and when they are approached by other network marketers to join their exciting, new company.

After discussing the company, go over the compensation plan. New distributors need to see how they can make money. They also need to be able to explain the plan to others. Go through the plan and ask the new distributors if they have questions. Then have them explain the plan to you. Praise and correct their attempt. Then have them explain it again and again, until they really understand and can clearly explain the plan. Compare your compensation plan with other types. For example, compare the breakaway, matrix, and binary plans discussed in Chapter 1. If you don't have this information, talk with your upline.

Next, discuss prospecting and recruiting. Talk about the importance of continually prospecting. Talk with them about the various prospecting techniques discussed in Chapter 5. Help new distributors select two or three prospecting methods they will commit to on a daily basis. Make up a plan of action, with times every day when they will prospect, plus goals for the number of new contacts they will make each day. Help them with a basic warm market call script. Role play this script until they are comfortable. Make some three-way calls with the new distributor, with you taking the lead and answering the tough questions.

Lastly, review the sign-up and training procedures for their new distributors. If you have done a good job of developing a duplicatable training program, this part will be very short because your new distributors will see how they can easily train their new distributors.

An initial training session should take no more than two hours. You must pack a great deal of information into a short period of time, so organize it ahead of time and stay on track. The new distributors should leave feeling confident that they can build a business and make money. Make sure you send them away with a plan of action, so they know what to do the next day. Call them that night to see how things went and answer questions. Remember to ask what you can do for them every time you call.

Never call your distributors to see how much they sold or how many people they recruited. They will feel as though you are their boss, and this will spoil your relationship. Set up a schedule for future trainings to include business operation, such as recordkeeping, bookkeeping, and taxes, retailing, recruiting, management, goal achievement, communications, and time planning. Develop outlines and handout materials for each of these trainings so that your distributors can then duplicate the strategies with their new distributors.

There is no better way to learn a business than to train other people. Training will create your leaders and drive your business into momentum growth. Prepare for it now. Develop a good, solid training program that is easily duplicatable and then present it consistently.

Chapter 10

The Beginning

Concluding a book on network marketing with a chapter on beginnings is fitting because you are beginning a new and exciting life. You have recognized that building networks is the way business will be conducted in the future, and you are ready to start building yours now.

All you have to do is find the people to fill your networks. Your mission is to find and help people prepare for the changing business environment.

Network marketing is not a little cottage industry anymore. It is one of the most dynamic, growth industries in the world today. Changing technology — from computers to transportation — are necessitating a change in the marketing and distribution of most products.

Go out and spread the word about your company, products and the industry. Don't worry about what people say or think. It doesn't matter, as long as you do the best job possible of presenting the message.

Think of yourself as just having entered network marketing college. During your first year or two, you will get your bachelor's degree. Continue for a couple more years and you can have a master's degree. Dedicate yourself to becoming a master network marketer. Read everything you can find on network marketing. Attend seminars, business briefings, and trainings until you are a master. Listen and watch training and presentation tapes. Listen to an audio tape at least 50 times, until you have it memorized. Study the top people in your company and the industry. What skills do they have that you don't? What beliefs, attitudes, and habits do they have? Find a mentor and practice mirroring him or her.

Develop some successful techniques and then practice them until they become rote. Use them with actual prospects or customers. Review the results and make adjustments. Repeat this process until you get the results you want.

Dedicate your life to contribution, rather than survival. You will become what you think about most. If you think about surviving — making it from paycheck to paycheck, never having enough time or money to do the things you want, that is all your life will become. On the other hand, if you commit to contribution, helping other people improve their lives through personal development, showing them how they can escape their survival lifestyle, that is what your life will become.

At this point, you have two choices, you can go on with your life as it is and hope for the best, or you can begin a new life. Remember that where you are today is the result of decisions you made five or ten years ago. Where you will be in five or ten years will be the result of decisions you make today.

Index

EXECARDS
Can Say It All!

Starting a network marketing business means building relationships that last a lifetime, and communication is the key to success. For instance, thanking a new customer for placing an order with you is an easy first step to building repeat sales and referrals. Select one of the following EXECARDS when it's time to say...

"Thank You"
"We Appreciate Your Business"
"Thanks For Your Order"
"We Welcome You As A New Customer"

Referrals and recruiting are the lifeblood of network marketing, and you can grow your business much faster by acknowledging sources and the accomplishments of people around you. EXECARDS let you say...

"Thanks For Your Referral"
"Thanks For Your Extra Effort"
"Welcome Aboard"

Whether you want to thank, encourage or congratulate, there's simply no better way to convey your professionalism than when you put it in writing.

You can also have your logo, company name or other message imprinted inside your EXECARDS for a small extra fee. There's no limit on imprinting.

EXECARDS®
1-800-228-2275

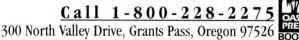

OASIS AUDIO CASSETTES

POWER MARKETING TOOLS FOR SMALL BUSINESS

featuring Jody Hornor

This helpful series provides 81 tools to increase your market power, as presented by Jody Hornor, author of *Power Marketing*. Plus two additional Power Marketing worksheets that will help you assess how you're doing and where to direct your marketing efforts.

This includes two cassette tapes, ideal for learning while traveling.

Power Marketing Tools For Small Business Cassette Tapes

$49.95
(two cassettes)

CALL 1-800-228-2275
to order or for more information

The Oasis Press®
Order Form

PSI Research. 300 North Valley Drive, Grants Pass, Oregon 97526 USA
Order Phone USA & Canada 1-800-228-2275
Inquiries & International Orders (541) 479-9464
FAX (541) 476-1479

Title	Binder	Paperback	Quantity	Cost
Customer Engineering	❑ $39.95	❑ $19.95		
How To Develop & Market Creative Business Ideas		❑ $14.95		
Know Your Market	❑ $39.95	❑ $19.95		
Marketing Mastery	❑ $39.95	❑ $19.95		
Power Marketing	❑ $39.95	❑ $19.95		
Starting & Operating A Business in... series book includes one federal section & one state. Please specify which state(s) you want:	❑ $29.95	❑ $24.95		
The Survey Genie Software (PC)		❑ $149.95		
Power Marketing Tools Cassette Tapes (2)		❑ $49.95		
TOTAL (see other side)				

For a complete catalog, with all of the small business books the Oasis Press® has to offer, call 1-800-228-2275.

OASIS PRESS BOOKS & SOFTWARE

SUB TOTAL (from other side)	
SHIPPING (see chart below)	
TOTAL ORDER	

If your purchase is:	Then your shipping is:
$0 - $25	$5.00
$25.01 - $50	$6.00
$50.01 - $100	$7.00
$100.01 - $175	$9.00
$175.01 - $250	$13.00
$250.01 - $500	$18.00
$500.01 +	4% of total purchase

ORDER MADE BY: (Please give your street address)

Name

Title

Company

Street Address

City/State/Zip

Daytime Phone

E-Mail

SHIP TO: (If different than above, give street address or P.O.Box)

Name

Title

Company

Address

City/State/Zip

Daytime Phone

BILLING INFORMATION (Rush service is available, please call)

❑ Check (Enclosed payable to PSI Research)

❑ Charge - ❑ Visa ❑ Mastercard ❑ Amex ❑ Discover

Card Number:

Expires:

Signature:

Name On Card:

Call toll free to order 1-800-228-2275

PSI Research   300 North Valley Drive, Grants Pass, OR 97526

FAX (541) 476-1479